Genetics and Genetic Services

A Child Welfare Workers' Guide

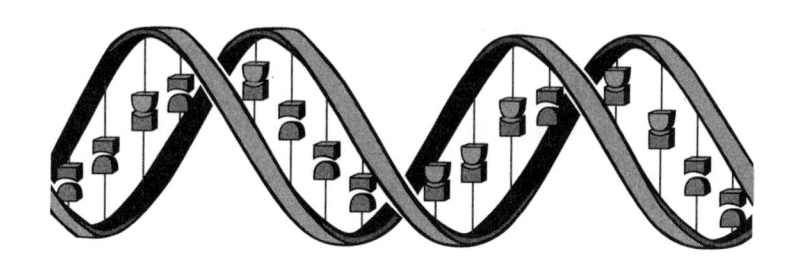

Karen Eanet & Julia B. Rauch

CWLA Press • Washington, DC

CWLA Press is an imprint of the Child Welfare League of America. The Child Welfare League of America (CWLA), the nation's oldest and largest membership-based child welfare organization, is committed to engaging all Americans in promoting the well-being of children and protecting every child from harm.

© 2000 by the Child Welfare League of America, Inc. All rights reserved. Neither this book nor any part may be reproduced or transmitted in any form or by any means, electronic or mechanical, including photocopying, microfilming, and recording, or by any information storage and retrieval system, without permission in writing from the publisher. For information on this or other CWLA publications, contact the CWLA Publications Department at the address below.

CHILD WELFARE LEAGUE OF AMERICA, INC.
440 First Street, NW, Third Floor, Washington, DC 20001-2085
E-mail: books@cwla.org

CURRENT PRINTING (last digit)
10 9 8 7 6 5 4 3 2 1

Cover design by Luke Johnson

Printed in the United States of America

ISBN # 0–87868-775-0

Library of Congress Cataloging-in-Publication Data
Eanet, Karen
    Genetics and genetic services: A child welfare workers' guide / Karen Eanet, Julia B. Rauch
      p. cm.
    Includes bibliographical references (p.   ).
    ISBN 0-87868-775-0 (alk. paper)
      1. Genetic counseling. 2. Genetic disorders in children--Patients--Services for--United States. 3. Child welfare workers. I. Rauch, Julia B. II. Title.
RB155.7.E24   2000   99-36504
616'.042--dc21   CIP

Contents

Quick References

Quick Reference #1: Criteria for Referral
    to Genetic Services vii
Quick Reference #2: How to Locate Genetic Services viii
Quick Reference #3: Information and Records
    Needed for Genetic Evaluations ix
Quick Reference #4: Birth Defects and Harmful
    Environmental Agents x
Quick Reference #5: Carrier Risks by Ethnic Group xiv
Quick Reference #6: Common Genetic Conditions xv

Foreword xxi
Acknowledgments xxiii
Introduction xxv

I. Introduction to Genetics and Genetic Services 1

1   Why Are Genetic Family Histories Important? 3
2   Selected Genetic Concepts 23
3   Genetic Services 31
4   Referrals to Genetic Services 35
5   Conducting the History-Taking Interview 43
6   Obtaining the Genetic Family History 49
7   Recording the Information 53
8   Transmitting the Information 65

II. Genetics and Child Welfare 69

9   Self-Awareness and Self-Directed Learning 71
10 Genetic Disorders and Child Development 87

11 Demands on Caregivers 97
12 Personal, Social, and Ethical Issues 111
13 Cultures, Co-cultures, and Genetics 119

Appendices

A Organizations 159
B Genetic Family History, Long Form 167
C Recommendations for Obtaining, Storing,
    and Transmitting Genetic Information 177
D Federal Information Centers and Clearinghouses 187
E Recommended Readings 191

References 201
About the Authors 209

Figures

Figure 1   Autosomal Dominant Inheritance 25
Figure 2   Autosomal Recessive Inheritance 26
Figure 3   X-Linked Recessive Inheritance 27
Figure 4   Maryland Health Passport: Child's Health History 54
Figure 5   Maryland Health Passport: Instructions 57
Figure 6   Symbols Used in a Pedigree Diagram 59
Figure 7   Directions for Drawing a Pedigree Diagram 60
Figure 8   Form for Recording a Pedigree Diagram 61
Figure 9   Example of a Completed Pedigree Diagram 63
Figure 10 Attitude Continuum 74
Figure 11 Learning Steps 79
Figure 12 Cultural Generalizations 126

Exercises

Exercise 1	What Do You Think About Genetics?	17
Exercise 2	Do You Want to Know About Faulty Genes?	21
Exercise 3	Your Family Genetic History	47
Exercise 4	Differentness Self-Awareness	81
Exercise 5	Your Genetic Disorders Biography	83
Exercise 6	Current Relationships	85
Exercise 7	Genetics and Cultural Change	151
Exercise 8	Communication Behaviors	153
Exercise 9	Your Intercultural Biography	154
Exercise 10	Some Genetics and Culture Self-Awareness Questions	156
Exercise 11	Interview Mindfulness Questions	158

Quick Reference #1:
Criteria for Referral to Genetic Services

Infants, Children, and Adolescents
- developmental delay or mental retardation
- birth defect or major physical anomaly, such as cleft lip/palate, clubfoot, extra or missing fingers, unusual body proportions
- major organ malformation, such as a congenital heart defect or a missing kidney
- complete or partial blindness or hearing loss
- loss or deterioration of motor, speech, or other capacities in a child who was previously thriving
- evidence of maternal drug or alcohol abuse during pregnancy, or of maternal infection with a sexually transmitted virus during pregnancy, or of maternal exposure to other viral, chemical, or radiological agents known or suspected of causing birth defects
- known or suspected hereditary disorder in the biological family

People of Reproductive Age
- a genetic disorder or birth defect in one partner
- previous child with a known or suspected genetic disorder
- maternal age of 35 years or older
- exposure to drugs, alcohol, infections, or chemical or radiological agents known or suspected of causing birth defects
- family history of known genetic disorder
- family history of known or suspected chromosome errors
- multiple early miscarriages or stillbirths
- members in an ethnic group known to have an incidence of specific genetic disorders higher than the general public
- known carrier of a gene for a genetic disorder
- anxiety about transmission of a familial disorder to offspring

Quick Reference #2:
How to Locate Genetic Services

1. Telephone your nearest medical school hospital. Ask for the genetic services department. Ask to speak to a genetic counselor.
2. Ask your (or your partner's) obstetrician.
3. Contact the National Clearinghouse for Maternal and Child Health. A staff member will be able to give you the names, addresses, phone numbers, and contact persons for genetic services in your state.

   National Maternal and Child Health Clearinghouse
   2070 Chain Bridge Road, Suite 450
   Vienna, VA 22182-2536
   888/434-4624, 703/356-1964
   Fax: 703/821-2098
   E-mail: nmchc@circsol.com
   www.nmchc.org

4. Contact the Alliance for Genetic Support Groups. Alliance staff will also be able to tell you about support groups and other resources in your area.

   Alliance of Genetic Support Groups
   4301 Connecticut Avenue NW, Suite 404
   Washington, DC 20008-2304
   800/336-4363, 202/966-5557
   Fax: 202/966-8553
   E-mail: info@geneticalliance.org
   www.geneticalliance.org

5. Contact the National Society of Genetic Counselors, which has a state-by-state referral list.

   National Society of Genetic Counselors, Inc.
   233 Canterbury Drive
   Wallingford, PA 19086-6617
   Tel: 610/872-7608
   E-mail: nsgc@aol.com
   www.nsgc.org
   www.pitt.edu/~edugene/resource (Genetic Resource Center)

Quick Reference #3:
Information and Records Needed
for Genetic Evaluations

When an appointment is made for a genetic evaluation, the genetic counselor will tell you what information and records are needed. The needed information will vary, depending on the reason for the evaluation. The items listed below are frequently requested, however, and should be available before, or at, the appointment.

- ethnic background of the person's parents and, if possible, grandparents
- individual's genetic family history
- prenatal care records
- birth records
- pediatric/medical care records
- hospitalization records
- any psychological, psychiatric, developmental delay or other evaluations
- medical/psychiatric/psychological records of first-degree relatives, particularly if there is evidence that the person was affected by a genetic disorder
- school records
- signed consent to medical procedures
- signed consent to photograph the individual, if requested

Quick Reference #4: Birth Defects and Harmful Environmental Agents

Certain chemicals and substances are known to cause birth defects to the developing fetus. Currently, 20–30 substances have been proven to cause birth defects in pregnancy. These substances are known as *teratogens*.

If you have a question about the effects of a particular drug, infection, or radiation exposure on the developing child, the March of Dimes Resource Center can provide information about specific teratogens and their effects. Contact the Center at 888/MODIMES (888/663-4637) or at www.modimes.org. In addition, most genetic counselors can answer questions about known or possible teratogens. Contact your nearest genetic center or the National Society of Genetic Counselors at 610/872-7608 or at www.nsgc.org.

General Features of Teratogens

Dosage and threshold effects: The effects of a specific teratogen may differ in different situations. Dose, duration, and frequency of exposure contribute to the nature, severity, and extent of damage. On the whole, most teratogens have no effect below specific levels, or thresholds. Heavy doses of most teratogens can be lethal for the developing fetus and the mother.

Timing: Some teratogens have their effects only during specific stages of prenatal development. Others can have effects throughout pregnancy. The first three months of pregnancy is the critical period of organ and limb development; brain development can be affected up through the last month of pregnancy.

Uncertainty: No teratogen causes birth defects 100% of the time; thus, it is not possible to predict with certainty whether a specific baby will be affected by a teratogen to which it was exposed.

Risk: Every woman has a 2–3% chance that she will have a baby born with some type of birth defect; exposure to a teratogen increases this risk, but it cannot be eliminated.

Some common teratogens include (not a comprehensive list) the following.

Congenital Infections

Cytomegalovirus: CMV is transmitted by sexual contact and secretions. Effects on the baby include hearing loss, a small head (microcephaly), mental retardation, visual defects, and dental anomalies. Infected adults may be symptom-free. About 1% of pregnant women are infected; only a small percentage of these will have affected babies.

HIV: Maternal HIV/AIDS is not associated with birth defects or mental retardation in the baby. If a mother is HIV or has AIDS, the biggest risk is that the virus will be passed on to the fetus. AZT treatment during pregnancy can greatly reduce the risk to the baby.

Syphilis: This is a sexually transmitted disease that can seriously harm the developing fetus. Half of infected pregnant women will miscarry. If the pregnancy survives, effects may include premature birth, anemia, jaundice, skin rash, mental retardation, blindness, and deafness. Some infected women will deliver healthy babies, however.

Toxoplasmosis: This infection is transmitted by contact with cat feces or raw meat. About 75% of infected fetuses will not have symptoms. Symptoms include prematurity, low birthweight, visual defects, mental retardation, and certain body abnormalities.

Other maternal infections that can potentially cause birth defects include chicken pox, rubella (German Measles), and exposure to Fifth disease (erythemia infectiosum).

Chemicals, Drugs, and Medications

Alcohol: The features of *fetal alcohol syndrome* (FAS) occur in 30%–40% of babies of women who are chronic alcoholics. Another 50%–70% may suffer from *fetal alcohol effects* (FAE). To be diagnosed with FAS, there must be a history of maternal alcohol abuse and a baby must have the following features:
- growth retardation
- central nervous system problems
- characteristic facial appearance: microcephaly (small head), flat facial profile, thin upper lip
- may have other major birth defects in internal organs, such as the heart and the digestive system

Children with FAS have failure to thrive, mild to moderate mental retardation, and behavior problems. The severity of FAE varies from very mild to severe. It often is associated with learning difficulties and attention-deficit/hyperactivity disorder. FAE is often overlooked as a cause of a child's problems and thus needed and appropriate services are not obtained.

Cigarette smoking: Constant exposure to cigarette smoke decreases the amount of oxygen crossing the placenta and can lead to low birthweight and premature birth.

Cocaine and other street drugs: Prenatal cocaine exposure does not appear to be associated with any particular birth defect or group of birth defects. Cocaine causes blood vessels to shrink and is associated with many prenatal complications, including miscarriage, placental abruption (separation of the placenta from the wall of the uterus), vascular defects, and in utero strokes.

Cocaine-exposed newborns may have withdrawal symptoms (be irritable, difficult to console, "shaky baby"). Cocaine-exposed babies are at risk for Sudden Infant Death Syndrome (SIDS). Researchers are looking at school-age children of women who used cocaine during pregnancy to determine the long-range effects, if any.

Women addicted to other street drugs are at increased risk for having babies born addicted to these drugs. The biggest risks to the babies are not from the drugs themselves, but from poor maternal nutrition and lack of prenatal care.

Anticonvulsants: Exposure to antiseizure medications is associated with *fetal anticonvulsant syndrome*. Approximately 10% of children exposed to dilantin and other seizure medications will have some growth and mental retardation, underdeveloped fingers, and a characteristic face. Exposure to valproic acid and carbamazepine are associated with a 1% risk for spina bifida.

Lithium: Exposure to lithium is associated with an increased risk for congenital heart defects. In addition, women who have bipolar disease may have an increased chance to have a child with the same condition. Family history is extremely important for determining risks in this situation.

Retinoids, vitamin A, and Accutane: Women taking oral Accutane have a high risk of having a baby with major birth defects, including fluid in the brain, a small head, mental retardation, malformed ears, facial abnormalities, and heart defects.

Physical Agents

Diagnostic x-rays: Routine x-ray exposure (dental x-rays, diagnostic x-rays) is not generally thought to cause birth defects. Large exposures, such as those seen in radiation therapy for cancer, may cause miscarriage early in pregnancy and affect fertility later in pregnancy.

Maternal Factors

Maternal Diabetes: Women who are diabetic are twice as likely as other women to have a baby with a birth defect. Possible defects include babies who are large for their gestational age or, more rarely, failure of the lower spine and limbs to form. The risk is reduced by better diabetic control during pregnancy.

Maternal Phenylketonuria (PKU) prior to and during pregnancy: Women with PKU who do not go on phenylalanine-restricted diets have a 90% risk of having a child with a small head and mental retardation. Diet restrictions prior to and during pregnancy can greatly improve the chances that the baby will be healthy.

Quick Reference #5:
Carrier Risks by Ethnic Groups

Members of certain ethnic groups carry genes for certain single gene conditions at higher rates than the population as a whole. Members of those groups who are considering having children may be interested in carrier screening. The condition, at-risk population, and approximate carrier frequency are listed below. To obtain brochures about the condition and carrier screening, contact the appropriate organization listed in Appendix A, Organizations.

Disease	At-Risk Population	Carrier Frequency
Sickle cell anemia	African Americans	1/10
Tay-Sachs disease	Eastern European Jews	1/25
	French Canadians	
α-Thalassemia	Greeks, Italians	1/30
β-Thalassemia	Southeast Asians	1/25
	Chinese	
Cystic fibrosis	Northern Europeans	1/20
	Eastern European Jews	1/30
Phenylketonuria	Northern Europeans	1/30

Quick Reference #6: Common Genetic Conditions

These are listed with at least one organization for obtaining additional information.

Achondroplasia
Incidence: 1/20,000 individuals
Inheritance: autosomal dominant, one half are new mutations
Features:
- skeletal dysplasia with extremely short stature
- normal intelligence

For more information:
Little People of America
888/LPA-2001
www.dwarfism.org

Bipolar Disorder (Manic Depression)
Incidence: occurs in about 17.4 million people in the United States
Inheritance: a few families have clearly dominant inheritance, other cases involve a combination of genetic predisposition and environmental factors
Features:
- Periods of depression: prolonged sadness, loss of energy, feelings of guilt and worthlessness
- Periods of mania: heightened mood, decreased need for sleep, irritability, aggression, reckless behaviors

For more information:
National Depressive and Manic-Depressive Association
800/826-3632
www.ndmda.org

Cystic fibrosis
Incidence: 1/2,500 Northern European Caucasians
Inheritance: autosomal recessive
Features:
- thick mucous in lungs and pancreas, leading to respiratory and digestive problems
- increased susceptibility to infection
- decreased fertility
- death in early adulthood, sometimes later

For more information:
Cystic Fibrosis Foundation
800/344-4823
www.cff.org

DiGeorge/Velo-cardio-facial syndrome
Incidence: 1/2000 individuals
Inheritance: chromosome 22 microdeletion, can be dominantly inherited
Features:
- cleft palate
- characteristic face
- congenital heart defect (interrupted aortic arch)
- mild to moderate mental retardation

For more information:
22q and You Center
215/590-2290
http://cbil.upenn.edu/VCFS/
index.html

Down syndrome

Incidence: 1/650 live births
Inheritance: chromosomal, 97% of cases are not inherited
Features:
- characteristic face
- mental retardation
- low muscle tone
- 50% have a congenital heart defect

For more information:
National Down Syndrome Society
800/221-4602
www.ndss.org

Duchenne muscular dystrophy

Incidence: 1/10,000 males
Inheritance: X-linked recessive
Features:
- progressive muscle weakness and hypertrophy
- wheelchair dependence by early teens
- early death due to respiratory failure

For more information:
Muscular Dystrophy Association
800/572-1717
www.mdausa.org

Familial hypercholesterolemia

Incidence: 1/500 carry one copy of the gene
Inheritance: autosomal dominant, with carriers having symptoms
Features:
- children with two copies of gene have extremely high levels of cholesterol and die in their 20s due to coronary artery disease
- individuals with one copy have high levels of cholesterol and have increased chance of early coronary artery disease by age 30

For more information:
Inherited High Cholesterol Project
888/244-2465
www.cholesterol.med.utah.edu

Fetal alcohol syndrome

Incidence: dependent on population, may be around 1/1,000 live births
Inheritance: seen in about 30-50% of infants of chronic alcoholic women
Features:
- characteristic face
- growth delay
- mental redardation

For more information:
National Organization on Fetal Alcohol Syndrome
202/785-4585
www.nofas.org

Fetal dilantin syndrome

Incidence: around 1/5,000 infants
Inheritance: seen in 10%–30% of infants exposed to dilantin (seizure medication) during pregnancy
Features:
- characteristic face
- hypoplastic (underdeveloped) fingernails

- some degree of mental retardation or learning disability

For more information:
National Organization for Rare Disorders
800/999-6673
www.rarediseases.org

Fragile X syndrome

Incidence: 1/1,000 males, 1/2,000 females
Inheritance: atypical X-linked inheritance
Features:
- most common inherited form of mental retardation in males, also affects females
- long face with large ears
- autisticlike behaviors

For more information:
National Fragile X Foundation
800/688-8765
www.nfxf.org

Gaucher disease

Incidence: 1/1,000 in Eastern European Jewish population
Inheritance: autosomal recessive
Features:
- enlargement of liver and spleen
- bone pain and swelling
- easily bruised
- symptoms vary greatly from individual to individual

For more information:
National Gaucher Foundation
800/925-8885
www.gaucherdisease.org

Hemophilia, type A

Incidence: 1/10,000 males
Inheritance: X-linked recessive
Features:
- easily bruised
- inability to clot
- heavy bleeding
- joint pain and swelling

For more information:
National Hemophilia Foundation
800/424-2634
www.hemophilia.org

Huntington's disease

Incidence: 1/3,000 individuals
Inheritance: autosomal dominant
Features:
- symptoms do not generally appear until after age 40
- ataxic (jerky) movements
- progressive mental deterioration

For more information:
Huntington's Disease Society of America
800/345-4372
www.hdsa.org

Marfan syndrome

Incidence: 1/15,000–20,000 individuals
Inheritance: autosomal dominant
Features:
- tall stature, with long arms and legs
- nearsightedness (myopia) with lens dislocation
- heart defects: enlarged aorta, mitral valve prolapse, aortic aneurysm
- family history of sudden death

For more information:
National Marfan Foundation
800/862-7326
www.marfan.org

Myotonic dystrophy
Incidence: 1/10,000 individuals
Inheritance: autosomal dominant
Features:
- variable progressive muscle weakness and stiffness
- droopy mouth, eyelids
- expressionless face
- cataracts
- congenital heart disease

For more information:
Muscular Dystrophy Association
800/572-1717
www.mdausa.org

Neurofibromatosis, type 1
Incidence: 1/5,000 individuals
Inheritance: autosomal dominant
Features:
- cafe-au-lait spots
- multiple neurofibromas (benign tumors under the skin)
- learning disabilities in about 25%

For more information:
Neurofibromatosis, Inc.
800/942-6825
www.nfinc.org

Noonan syndrome
Incidence: 1/5,000 individuals
Inheritance: autosomal dominant with many new mutations
Features:
- short stature
- congenital heart disease (pulmonic stenosis)
- learning disability to mild to moderate mental retardation

For more information:
The Noonan Syndrome Support Group, Inc.
888/686-2224
www.noonansyndrome.org

Phenylketonuria (PKU)
Incidence: 1/13,000 individuals
Inheritance: autosomal recessive
Features:
- one of the disorders on the newborn screen in most states
- children must be placed on phenylalanine-free diet for life
- untreated children will develop mental retardation and seizures
- women with PKU must be on diet during pregnancy

For more information:
Children's PKU Network
619/233-3202
E-mail: pkunetwork@aol.com
(no Internet site)

Schizophrenia
Incidence: occurs in about 2 million people in the United States
Inheritance: a few families have dominantly inherited disease; most cases are a result of genetic factors and other unknown influences.
Features:
- Psychotic symptoms: hallucinations, delusions
- Disorganized symptoms: confused thinking and speech
- Negative symptoms: emotional flatness, lack of expression

For more information:
National Alliance for the Mentally Ill
800/950-6264
www.nami.org

Sex chromosome abnormalities

Includes Turner syndrome (45 X), Klinefelter syndrome (47 XXY), 47 XYY, 47 XXX
<u>Incidence</u>: 1/500–1,000 live births
<u>Inheritance</u>: chromosomal, not generally inherited
<u>Common features:</u>
- short stature in Turner syndrome, tall stature in Klinefelter syndrome
- learning disabilities
- not generally mentally retarded
- infertility

For more information:
Klinefelter Syndrome and Associates
916/773-2999
www.genetic.org
Turner's Syndrome Society of the United States
800/365-9944
www.turner-syndrome-us.org

Sickle cell anemia

<u>Incidence</u>: 1/600 African Americans
<u>Inheritance</u>: autosomal recessive
<u>Features:</u>
- increased susceptibility to infection
- sickle cell crises (swelling of joints, pain)
- enlargement of spleen
- anemia

For more information:
Sickle Cell Disease Association of America
800/421-8453
www.sicklecelldisease.org

Stickler syndrome

<u>Incidence</u>: 1/20,000 individuals
<u>Inheritance</u>: autosomal dominant
<u>Features:</u>
- cleft palate with small jaw
- nearsightedness (myopia)
- retinal detachment
- early arthritis in 20s or 30s

For more information:
Stickler Involved People
316/775-2993
www.sticklers.org

Tay-Sachs disease

<u>Incidence</u>: 1/3,600 in Eastern European Jewish population, 1/50,000 in general population (rarely seen because of widespread genetic screening)
<u>Inheritance</u>: autosomal recessive
<u>Features:</u>
- progressive neurological degeneration
- death by age 3–5 years

For more information:
National Tay-Sachs and Allied Diseases Association
800/906-8723
www.ntsad.org

Thalassemia (alpha and beta)

<u>Incidence</u>: 1/3,000 beta-thal in Mediterranean populations, alpha-thal in Asian population

Inheritance: autosomal recessive
Features:
- moderate to severe anemia
- increased susceptibility to infections
- increased risk for fetal death

For more information:
Cooley's Anemia Foundation, Inc./
    Thalessemia Action Group
    Support Group
800/522-7222
www.thalassemia.org

Trisomy 13, 18

Incidence: 1/3,000–5000 live births
Inheritance: chromosomal, not generally inherited
Features:
- severe birth defects
- death in by age 1
- profound mental retardation in survivors

For more information:
Support Organization for Trisomy 18, 13, and Related Disorders
800/716-7638
www.trisomy.org

VATER (VACTERL) Association

Incidence: 1/3,000–5,000 live births
Inheritance: sporadic, not generally inherited
Nonrandom association of birth defects:
- vertebral anomalies
- anal atresia
- cardiac defects
- tracheoesophageal fistula
- renal and limb anomalies

For more information:
TEF/VATER/VACTERL National
    Support Network
301/952-6837
www.rarediseases.org

Williams syndrome

Incidence: 1/5,000 individuals
Inheritance: chromosome 7 microdeletion, can be dominantly inherited
Features:
- characteristic face and personality
- moderate mental retardation
- congenital heart disease/supravalvular aortic stenosis

For more information:
Williams Syndrome Association
800/806-1871
www.williams-syndrome.org

Foreword

Child welfare workers serve some of America's most vulnerable families and children. One aspect of this vulnerability is their emotional, mental, and physical health. A serious necessity in child welfare is for more attention to be paid to children's health needs in terms of identification, documentation, and service provision.

Genetics and Genetic Services: A Child Welfare Workers' Guide helps meet this need by informing workers of the importance of genetic family histories for children in their care and by teaching the "how to's" of taking a genetic family history. Since many significant medical problems can be traced through family lines, knowledge of genetic conditions that have affected relatives for generations can enable workers, families, and children themselves, as adults, to make more informed treatment decisions regarding their health. Given the chaos in many of the lives of children in the child welfare system, early documentation of their genetic health histories is important before such information is lost forever.

One of the most precious gifts we can give a child is a documented history of his/her family's health. This guide can help child welfare workers ensure that this gift is presented.

Christina Ripley-Curtiss, M.S.W., Ph.D.
Associate Professor and
Doctoral Program Director
Arizona State University

Acknowledgments

We are indebted to many people for their support, encouragement, and assistance. The idea for a guide to genetics and genetic services for child welfare workers first emerged in meetings of the Maryland Ad Hoc Interprofessional Committee on Genetics and Adoption. Members who participated in formulating the idea were Craig Adams, Barbara Bernhardt, Joan Cooper, the late Lillian Lansberry, Dawn Musgrave, Susan Noel, Nancy Rike, Marion Robertson, and Virginia White.

The Ad Hoc Committee was continuing work that began in a mid-Atlantic regional conference on genetics and adoption held in May 1990 under the auspices of the Mid-Atlantic Regional Human Genetics Network, with support from the Genetics Services Branch of the U.S. Public Health Service, Health Resources and Services Administration, Maternal and Child Health Bureau. Local chapters of the March of Dimes Birth Defects Foundation also provided stipends for individuals from their localities to attend the conference. For their support of the regional conference, we thank Steven Amato, Louis Bartoshesky, Joanne Bodurtha, Germaine Bowles, Franklin Desposito, Juanita Devine, Edward Duffy, Christine Estlake, Thaddeus Kelly, Brenda Kerr, Carol King, Margie Lance, and the late Elaine Schwartz

This guide has two direct ancestors. One was a brief, unpublished guide to genetics and genetic services in Maryland that was written by Julia B. Rauch and Nancy Rike, which the Maryland Department of Human Resources distributed to child welfare workers throughout the state. Subsequently, the guide was edited to delete Maryland-specific content and was distributed by Spaulding for Children. Thanks to Drenda Lakin.

The second ancestor was *Taking a Family Health/Genetic History: An Ethnocultural Learning Guide and Handbook*. Again with support from the Genetic Services Branch, *Taking a Family Health/Genetic History: An Ethnocultural Learning Guide and Handbook* was written to support

Maryland-wide training for child welfare workers in genetics and genetic services, using a multicultural perspective. It was distributed through the National Maternal and Child Health Clearinghouse and the Child Welfare League of America. Thanks for their support to Jeanne Athey, Kathleen Kirk Bishop, Jennie Bloom, Joann Boughman, Eloise Bridges, Sue Brocklebank, Jan Butts, Maria Carter, Paul Ephross, Juanita Evans, Alicia Fairley, Marianne Felice, Geoffrey Greif, Muriel Grey, Rebecca Hegar, Lisa Higdon, Steven Howe, Larke Nahme Huang, Jamie Israel, Leonard T. Jackson, Carl Kendall, Archie Lynch, Ilana Mittman, Florence Neal-Cooper, Carolyn North, Julianne Oktay, Susan Panny, Patricia Powers, Christina Risley-Curtiss, Marion Robertson, Cyprian Rowe, Robert Stevens, the late Elaine Schwartz, Stuart Swayze, Rita Webb, Stanley Wenocur, Eric Wulfsburg, and Ronald Zuskin. The current guide contains a form for obtaining and recording family health/genetic histories that was developed for Maryland's child welfare workers (Appendix B). People involved in this effort were Barbara Bernhardt, Karen Hofman, the late Lillian Lansberry, Julia B. Rauch, Leslie Raffle, Nancy Rike, and Susan Weigel.

This guide can be considered as an expansion and revision of the previous efforts. We particularly thank the following for their help with this revision: Miriam Blitzer, Caroline Burry, Jean Christensen, Maimon Cohen, Tammy Derry, Luba Djurdjinovic, Jesse J. Harris, Richard Norman, Edward Pecukonis, Patricia Peiper, and Eric Wulfsburg. Susan Brite, of the Child Welfare League of America, was more than patient. Thanks also to our editor, Cathy Corder.

Karen Eanet
Julia B. Rauch

Introduction

Human genetics deals with those qualities that distinguish human beings from other species and that differentiate populations, families, and individuals from each other. Genetic scientists study the causes of hereditary similarities and differences, ways in which they pass from generation to generation, and factors that affect gene expression. Medical genetics is concerned with the causes, prevention, diagnosis, and treatment of genetic disorders in humans. This guide focuses on medical genetics, including psychosocial aspects of genetic disorders.

Genetic disorders appear as chronic illnesses, such as sickle cell disease or cystic fibrosis, and as varied disabilities, such as cognitive (mental retardation), sensory (blindness), physical (cerebral palsy), and behavioral (schizophrenia).

Many thousands of inherited diseases have been identified [McKusick 1999]. Before the age of 25, 53 of 1,000 live-born individuals will have a disease with a genetic component. Fifty percent of all conceptions are lost for genetic reasons before the pregnancy is recognized; one in 15 of recognized pregnancies miscarries for genetic reasons. Genetic disorders account for 40% of infant deaths and 30% of pediatric hospital admissions [Rimoin et al. 1996; Robinson 1988]. Later in life, genetically influenced cardiovascular disease, hypertension, Alzheimer's disease, and cancers exact their tolls [Pyeritz 1989]. Research evidence suggests that schizophrenia, mood disorders, and certain other psychiatric illnesses are influenced by genetic factors [McGuffin & Murray 1991; McGuffin et al. 1994].

Inherited conditions, however, are only one category of genetic disorders. Other categories are chromosome anomalies and disorders caused by exposure to harmful environmental agents before and/or after birth. As you can see, genetic disorders are a major public health problem.

Advances in medical technology and improved treatments have increased the life expectancy of people with genetic disorders. Individuals who once would have died in infancy or childhood are living to adulthood [Rimoin et al. 1996, p. 35]. Thus, the number of infants, children, and adolescents with genetic disorders is increasing. Because children with chronic illnesses and disabilities are more likely than other children to enter the child welfare system, the incidence of genetic disorders is probably higher among children in child welfare caseloads than among other children. We decided to write this guide because we believe that children under child welfare supervision should have the benefit of access to genetic services. We believe, too, that adult graduates of out-of-home care and adult adoptees have the right to their biological families' health histories.

This guide is intended for child welfare workers and other human services providers involved with children who are under child welfare supervision. Its goals are to encourage

- the acquisition of a genetic family history for each child under child welfare supervision and each child eligible for adoption,
- better utilization of genetic services for children under child welfare supervision,
- more effective psychosocial interventions with children affected by genetic disorders and their caregivers, and
- appropriate balancing of the confidentiality of genetic information with others' right to know.

To achieve these goals, child welfare workers need to know about the following:

- their feelings about people who are "different" and how those feelings may affect their behavior;
- their feelings about medical genetics and genetic services and how those feelings may affect their behavior;
- the role of genetic information in child welfare;
- the causes of genetic disorders;
- available genetic services and how to locate and utilize them;
- how to obtain and record genetic family histories;

- how to balance the confidentiality of genetic information with others' rights or needs to know;
- the impact of genetic disorders on child development;
- demands experienced by caregivers of infants, children, and adolescents with genetic disorders;
- dilemmas of being at genetic risk and making decisions about having biological children;
- legal and ethical issues of genetic information in child welfare; and
- genetic information, genetic services, and people from diverse cultural backgrounds.

The guide begins with a set of quick references that you can use when you need handy, practical information about obtaining genetic services for a specific client. The quick references cover criteria for referral to genetic services, how to locate genetic services, information and records needed for genetic evaluations, environmental agents that may cause birth defects, carrier risks by ethnic group, and some common genetic disorders. These quick references should help you to assess if a specific client might benefit from a genetic service, and to access and utilize the appropriate genetic service.

The guide has both genetic/technical and psychosocial content. Part I conveys genetic information. The first chapter reviews the reasons why genetic family histories are important for children under child welfare supervision, including those eligible for adoption. The second chapter summarizes selected genetic concepts. The third describes current genetic services. The *how* of referring a child for genetic evaluation is discussed in Chapter 4. Some techniques for conducting a genetic family history-taking interview are covered in Chapter 5. Chapter 6 looks at different strategies for obtaining genetic family history information. Chapter 7 discusses the recording of genetic information and Chapter 8, its transmission to others.

Part II provides content pertinent to psychosocial intervention with infants, children, and adolescents affected by genetic disorders, including aspects of referrals to prospective adoptive parents. It includes chapters on self-awareness about differentness (Chapter 9), the impact of genetic disorders on child development (Chapter 10), demands on caregivers (Chapter 11), and personal, social, and ethical issues of genetic information and reproductive decisionmaking (Chapter 12). The final chapter reviews dimensions of cultural diversity that are relevant to working with families of diverse backgrounds around genetic issues.

This guide includes several exercises intended to stimulate your thinking about these issues. We hope you will complete these exercises, which are incorporated into the text. The questions have no easy answer; however, they point out the difficult social and ethical issues associated with genetic information. We also hope that you will discuss some of the questions on the exercises with your significant others, friends, and colleagues so that you can sort out your own feelings and beliefs.

The guide has five appendices. They include a list of selected organizations concerned with genetic disorders; an example of a form for obtaining and recording a genetic family history; recommendations for obtaining, storing, and transmitted genetic information (formulated by a group of child welfare workers and genetic professionals); a list of selected federal information centers and clearinghouses; and a brief annotated bibliography.

I

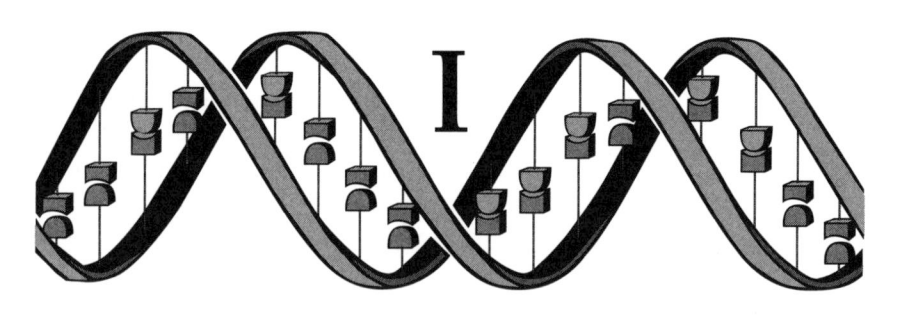

Introduction to Genetics and Genetic Services

Chapter 1

Why Are Genetic Family Histories Important?

A revolution in human genetics is occurring. The Human Genome Project (HGP), an international effort to identify all the estimated 100,000 genes by 2010, is under way and ahead of schedule. It is anticipated that all human genes will be identified by 2005 [Collins 1996].

The HGP is already making it possible for scientists to locate and study genes that cause specific disorders. Once scientists know what a gene does (or does not do), they probably will be able to develop better ways of preventing and treating genetic disorders. That, at least, is the *promise* of the genetic revolution [Engel 1993; Guyer & Collins 1993]. Many complex ethical, legal, and social dilemmas associated with the HGP provide an important context for you as you learn and think about human genetics and child welfare.

In this chapter, we talk about genetic family histories (GFHs). GFHs are currently the primary source of genetic information for children under child welfare supervision. We present the reasons why it is important for child welfare workers to obtain GFHs for children in their caseloads, when obtainable. Don't forget the context, however—the genetics revolution. Today's issues of genetic information in child welfare may be even more complex tomorrow than they are today.

Why Are Genetic Family Histories Important?

Genetic family histories are important for children in out-of-home care or who have been adopted, for several reasons.

To promote good health and health care throughout life

Many common health problems, such as heart disease, allergies, diabetes, obesity, and cancer, are caused by the interaction of inherited genes and lifestyles. We can't improve our health by changing our genes—at least not yet. We can, however, manage our lifestyles. If someone has a genetic predisposition for a certain disorder, a healthy lifestyle may delay its onset, make it less severe, and, possibly (depending on the specific condition), prevent symptoms from occurring.

Genetic family histories provide information that can be used to make health-related lifestyle decisions. They tell people which, if any, health problems run in their families. The histories inform people that they are "at risk"—more likely than other people—to develop a particular health problem. Knowing this, at-risk individuals can take preventive action.

> Mike L. knew that his maternal grandfather, mother, and older brother had late onset diabetes. Although he had a sweet tooth, he controlled his sugar intake and generally adhered to a diet recommended for the control of diabetes. At age 70, he has no symptoms of diabetes.

Just as Mike L. took preventive action on his own behalf, caretakers can take preventive action on behalf of children who are genetically at risk.

> When Mr. and Mrs. L. adopted Jun-Ling, the adoption worker informed them that Jun-Ling had a strong family history of asthma. As a precaution, Mr. and Mrs. L. replaced most of their carpeting with hardwood floors, bought a vacuum cleaner with a special filter, and got rid of their plants. After Jun-Ling's first birthday, a pediatric specialist in diseases of the lungs diagnosed mild asthma. At age 3, Jun-Ling is on medication for her asthma but is relatively free of symptoms, in part because she lives in a scrupulously clean environment.

To help doctors provide better medical care to children who are adopted or in out-of-home care during childhood and when they are adults

GFHs help doctors to provide better medical care. GFHs are particularly important for children under child welfare supervision because of evidence that these children have higher incidences of physical and mental health problems than do other children [Chadwick 1992; Chernoff et al. 1994; Carrasco 1999]. The information can help doctors make accurate diagnoses if a child develops symptoms of a chronic condition.

Diagnosing is often difficult because some symptoms have genetic *and* nongenetic causes in different people. For example, several inherited conditions cause blindness. If inherited, the blindness may be congenital (present at birth) or appear later in life. Blindness may also have other, noninherited causes, such as maternal German measles (rubella) during pregnancy, certain procedures used in neonatal intensive care nurseries to keep prematurely born babies alive, or head and eye injuries.

When a child has symptoms that may have genetic or nongenetic causes, GFHs provide clues as to whether or not the condition is genetic. The diagnosis has implications for medical care and psychosocial intervention.

> Sarah was adopted from an orphanage in Russia, where she was placed because her mother, who was alcoholic, was unable to care for her. Sarah was born with a cleft lip and palate, which is sometimes inherited. Sarah's adoptive parents were told that this was Sarah's only problem. Sarah had surgery to correct her cleft. However, Sarah remained small for her age and ate poorly. At around age 3, her parents noticed delayed speech development, but this was attributed to the cleft.
>
> When Sarah started school, she began to have behavior problems. It became clear that she had a learning disability and developmental delay. On the advice of Sarah's speech therapist, Sarah was taken to see a medical geneticist. After a review of Sarah's history and a careful physical exam, the geneticist diagnosed fetal alcohol effects. After this diagnosis, Sarah's parents

> **Importance of Genetic Family Histories**
> - To promote good health and good health care throughout life.
> - To help doctors provide better medical care to children who are adopted or in out-of-home care during childhood, and when they are adults.
> - To aid in early identification and diagnosis of behavioral or learning problems for which a child may be at risk.
> - To aid in social work assessment and intervention.
> - To give adult adoptees or graduates of out-of-home care information they can use to make reproductive decisions.
> - To prevent adoption disruption and dissolution and wrongful adoption suits.
> - To provide information that potential adoptive families can use in deciding whether they can parent a particular child.
> - To comply with changing adoption law, regulations, and standards.

arranged appropriate schooling for her, obtained guidance on home management, and joined a support group for adoptive parents of children with fetal alcohol effects.

Genetic family histories also aid doctors when a condition is known to run in a family. They can monitor their patients for signs of the family health problem. Chances for early, accurate diagnosis and timely treatment are increased.

If the gene for the condition has been identified, and a genetic test is available, testing to determine whether a person has the gene is possible. For example, it is possible to test some daughters of women with breast cancer to determine if they have mutations in either the BRCA1 or BRCA2 gene. Mutations in these genes increase a woman's risk to develop breast cancer.

Ms. P's mother died of breast cancer at age 34. Her two aunts and grandmother also had breast cancer. Knowing that she was at risk, Ms. P. had her first mammogram when she was 21, well below the recommended age for such testing. When she was 28, a mammogram revealed cancer in her left breast. A lumpectomy successfully removed the cancer, which had not spread. Now 39 years old, she has had no recurrence. Ms. P. is grateful that she knew about her risk and that her cancer was diagnosed early.

The genetic family history can also help doctors to choose the best treatment. For example, if allergy to penicillin runs in a family, the doctor is likely to choose another drug to fight a bacterial infection.

To aid in early identification and diagnosis of behavioral or learning problems for which a child may be at risk

Learning disabilities can have devastating effects if they are not recognized and appropriate services are not provided. Children with learning disabilities may fail repeatedly in school. Such a failure cycle may lead to emotional and behavioral problems, even in children with stable family lives. What price do these children pay when they are additionally traumatized by neglect, abuse, or separation from their biological parents?

Identifying the causes of learning disabilities or other behavioral problems is not easy. Remember, the same symptom or cluster of symptoms can have different causes in different people. When a child has a learning or behavioral problem, GFH information can point to the correct diagnosis, even if the information is incomplete or stated in lay language.

Mr. and Mrs. B. were foster parents for Benjamin, age 4, a shy, nervous child. At their caseworker's suggestion, they brought Benjamin to a genetics center for a genetics/developmental evaluation. They feared that Benjamin was mentally retarded and stated that they could not take care of a child who was going to be mentally retarded or mentally ill. They reported that Benjamin had to touch all objects and cried if stopped. He also held his head in a funny way. His biological mother, who had several hospitalizations for serious depression, reported that Benjamin's father was "weird" and "always making faces" and that he "smiles funny and says stuff he shouldn't say." This information enabled the geneticist to diagnose Benjamin as having Tourette's Syndrome, an inherited, debilitating tic disorder that may also be associated with attention difficulties, obsessions, and compulsions.

Sometimes the diagnostic picture is clouded because of a child's damaging life circumstances. Many if not most children in out-of-home care are emotionally scarred due to the neglect, abuse, abandonment, or other trauma preceding their entry into the child welfare system. Thus, it is tempting to blame learning, behavioral, or emotional problems entirely on early life experience. A wholly environmentalist mind-set, however, may cause biological factors to be overlooked. The result may be faulty assessments and inappropriate interventions. In the worse case scenario, the child may be harmed, or harm others.

> Vanessa was placed in the G. family foster home when she was 6 months old, after her biological mother, who had bipolar disorder, committed suicide. Mr. and Mrs. G. decided that they were interested in adopting Vanessa but wondered if Vanessa might also become manic depressive. The adoption worker assured Mr. and Mrs. G. that psychiatric problems were not inherited and that Vanessa would do well if raised in a loving home. Vanessa was okay until third grade, when her teacher reported that she was hyperactive and had difficulty concentrating. At home, she became argumentative and prone to temper tantrums. She received two years of psychotherapy with an analytically oriented child psychiatrist who attributed her problems to anger at losing her mother.

> Despite therapy, Vanessa's behavior only worsened. The by-then desperate parents sought family therapy. The family therapist felt that marital tensions between Mr. and Mrs. G. were being "detoured" through Vanessa. Thus, Vanessa was seen as manifesting a family pathology. Family therapy, too, did not help.

Vanessa increasingly became a "Dr. Jekyll and Ms. Hyde," compliant one minute, angry and unpredictable the next. When she was 14, Vanessa attempted suicide and was hospitalized in the adolescent psychiatry unit of a university medical center. Learning that Vanessa's biological mother had bipolar disorder, the psychiatrist realized that Vanessa, too, was affected by manic depression. He prescribed lithium, to which she responded well. Vanessa's condition is now stabilized and she is doing well at home, in school, and with peers.

To aid in social work assessment and intervention

Genetic family histories can aid in social work assessment and intervention planning [Bernhardt & Rauch 1993]. In child welfare, it is particularly important that assessments include screening for depression and other affective disorders [Rauch et al. 1991]. In many cases, depression or related affective (mood) disorders may contribute to the problems that bring children and families to the attention of child welfare agencies.

A neighbor reported to Child Protective Services that Ms. D., a young single parent, neglected and abused her little boy. When she visited the home, the CPS worker discovered Ms. D. in bed, even though it was noon. Mike, 3, was lying on the floor in a pile of dirty clothes, sucking his thumb, near some feces. There was no food in the house. Mike's arms, legs, and body were bruised. When the worker asked Ms. D. about other family members, Ms. D. reported that her mother and her sister each had histories of depression and psychiatric hospitalization. After arranging for Mike to go to a shelter, the worker took Ms. D. to an emergency room. The psychiatrist diagnosed Ms. D. as clinically depressed and hospitalized her. Ms. D. responded well to antidepressant medication, education about depression, supportive counseling, and participation in a self-help group for people with affective disorders. Ms. D. and Mike are now reunited, and Mike is thriving.

Neglect and abuse both may result from depression. Similarly, substance abuse may be a form of self-medication for depression. Depression and other affective disorders in children and adolescents may be expressed though an inability to concentrate, learning difficulties, and behavior problems [Rauch et al. 1991].

> Paul R., 14, lived with his maternal grandparents after his mother died of AIDS when he was 2 years old. He loved elementary school and had excelled academically. When he entered middle school, however, his grades dropped sharply. He began to hang out with older boys who were involved in drugs, and he began to use drugs himself. The police arrested him for drug dealing. The judge referred him to a model program for delinquent youth. The program's social worker learned that Paul's paternal grandfather had sharp mood swings and that his maternal aunt had several hospitalizations for clinical depression. The worker referred Paul to a psychiatrist. Based on the family history, the psychiatrist hypothesized that Paul's behavior indicated a mood disorder. He prescribed antidepressants, to which Paul responded well. As his mood lifted, Paul was able to take advantage of the counseling and mentoring offered by the model program. Eight months later, he is again excelling academically and hopes to go to college. He is a volunteer tutor of younger children in a community after-school program.

To plan effective interventions, child welfare workers need to be able to identify when depression or other affective disorders may be contributing to families' problems. A family history of depression, bipolar disorder, substance abuse, or violence should alert you to the possibility that the individual has depression or another affective disorder. The depression or other disorder may be contributing to—even causing—a family's troubles. Fortunately, in most cases affective disorders can be successfully treated.

Genetic family histories can aid in assessment and intervention in other ways. They can help you to "listen with the genetic ear" [Bishop 1993]. The GFH may suggest that a person may have an unstated genetic concern.

Mrs. S. reported that she was at her wit's end trying to cope with her niece, Sharon, 17. Sharon had lived with Mrs. S. since Sharon was 10, when her mother died of breast cancer, as had her grandmother. Sharon was doing poorly at school and hanging out with a "bad crowd." She had been arrested for shoplifting and had stayed out all night several times. Mrs. S. feared that Sharon was involved in drugs. The child welfare worker referred Sharon to a community mental health center for therapy. After their relationship was well-established, the therapist wondered if Sharon feared that, like her mother and grandmother, she would get breast cancer and die young. Sharon burst into tears, saying that she felt "doomed."

To give adult adoptees or graduates of foster care information that they can use to make reproductive decisions

Many adult adoptees and graduates of out-of-home care want information about their biological families. One reason is that they desire to have biological children but fear that a serious inherited disorder in their biological families might be transmitted to their children. Usually, GFHs relieve such anxieties.

If an individual learns that there is a serious genetic disorder in his or her family, genetic counselors can provide information about the disorder, the chances that it will be passed on to children, and what genetic services are available and appropriate. If the news is bad, the counselor can help the individual or couple to consider the available options.

Ms. M., who had been adopted at birth, was planning to marry Mr. J. She knew that two of her biological uncles on her mother's side had had hemophilia. She and Mr. J. met with a genetic counselor. The counselor described hemophilia, its treatment, prognosis, and inheritance. The counselor also said that a test could determine whether Ms. M. carried the gene for hemophilia. The test revealed that Ms. M. was a carrier; thus, there was a 50/50 chance that any of her sons might be affected. The counselor also stated that prenatal diagnosis was available. After considering their options, Ms. M. and Mr. J. decided that if Ms. M. became pregnant with a male child, she would have prenatal diagnosis so that her obstetrician could be prepared to handle the child's birth if the baby had hemophilia. They would not terminate the pregnancy. They believed that continuing advances in treating hemophilia effectively would ensure that any son with hemophilia would lead a healthy, relatively normal life.

To prevent adoption disruption and dissolution and wrongful adoption suits

The tragedy of adoption disruption and dissolution occurs for many reasons. Sometimes, however, adoption fails because the adoption agency did not provide important information [Kadushin & Martin 1988]. Adoptive parents have sued agencies after their children developed symptoms of such conditions as fetal alcohol effects and childhood schizophrenia. The suits have alleged that the agencies did not provide adequate information about the biological mother and her family. U.S. and Canadian courts have upheld the claims of wrongful adoption on grounds of intentional misrepresentation, deliberate concealment, and negligent disclosure [Andrews 1987; DeWoody 1993a, 1993b; Kopels 1995].

Another potential category of liability is negligently withholding material information regarding a child's history or prognosis—for example, failing to provide accurate information about the risks that a child may be affected by a genetic disorder [DeWoody 1993a]. In the future, courts may hold agencies responsible for obtaining GFHs and indicated genetic services [Kopels 1995].

Adoption disruption or dissolution and wrongful adoption suits are likely to further harm children who already may be traumatized. Providing a genetic family history can help the parents prepare to meet a child's special needs and increase the chances that an adoption will be successful.

To provide information that potential adoptive families can use in deciding whether they can parent a particular child

The genetic family history may suggest that a child has a genetic disorder or is at risk for developing a late onset condition, behavioral problem, or developmental disability. Using this information, prospective adoptive parents can decide whether or not they would be able to meet the child's special needs. Sometimes the GFH may lead potential parents to choose not to adopt a child. This would be unfortunate, of course, but as discussed above, withholding information may also be harmful. In addition, the authors believe that adoptive parents have a right to the fullest possible information when making such as important decision. The Child Welfare League of America's (CWLA) *Standards for Adoption Service* [CWLA 1988] stipulate full disclosure:

0.9 Self-determination and informed consent

Respect should be given for the right of all parties in adoption to self-determination and for the right to make decisions to the degree to which they are able and such decisions are feasible.

To make decisions and provide informed consent to place, or to add to the family via adoption, birth and adoptive parents should receive full and complete information from the agency pertinent to that decision. [p. 4]

Guidelines for preparing parents are available [Hockman & Huston 1994]. Recommendations for transmitting genetic information (jointly formulated by a group of child welfare staff and genetic counselors) appear in Appendix C.

To comply with changing adoption law and regulations

Openness of information in adoptions is one of the most controversial issues in the field. Nonetheless, the trend is toward requiring that the records of a child who is adopted include a genetic family history. CWLA's standards regarding children's health histories [1988, pp. 26-28] are excerpted on pages 14 and 15.

3.2 Medical Examination

A medical examination should be conducted by a qualified physician (preferably a pediatrician) to determine the state of the child's health, any known or potentially significant factors that may interfere with normal development, and the implications of any medical problems.

The following should be taken into consideration:

- An evaluation of the infant that includes a correlation and interpretation of all available information (e.g., genetic information, laboratory data);
- A complete pediatric examination of the older child, in accordance with the standards of the American Academy of Pediatrics, that includes the child's birth family and developmental history;
- The nature and degree of any existing handicap; complete information about the type of handicap and the concomitant treatment and support programs that should be provided to the child and adoptive parents; extra costs of medical care that can be anticipated; and plans to subsidize the health care, if so indicated;
- The adoptive parents' need for access to medical consultation for any child they are considering adopting.

3.4 Family history

Information should be obtained from the birth mother and father about their family backgrounds:

- To determine whether there are any significant hereditary factors or pathology, including illnesses of the birth mother or father, that may affect the child's development;

- To help the adoptive parents and eventually the child understand the family situation, the reasons for adoptions, and the birth family histories;
- To decide, in the case of older children who have lived with their birth families, which characteristics should be given consideration in selecting and preparing for a new family.

State adoption laws vary on what information should be collected, who should collect it, to whom it can be disclosed, and the disclosure procedures. As of September 1992, adoption law in 18 states required that genetic family histories be collected [DeWoody 1993b]. In at least one state (Maryland), the judicial definition of *medical record* requires a genetic family history, if obtainable [Judge Peter J. Messite in a 1992 letter to Julia Rauch]. The Uniform Adoption Act (see box on page 16), approved by the National Conference of Commissioners on Uniform State Laws in 1994, specifies disclosure to prospective adoptive parents of a child's genetic family history, as well as other information [Blair 1996].

In December 1995, the Children's Bureau convened a group of national, state, and local representatives of adoption organizations who recommended a national strategic planning goal: Children, families, and network partners will have access to all information pertinent to meeting the needs of the adopted child [National Adoption Strategic Plan 1996].

In the future, adoption agencies and professionals will increasingly be expected to meet the following responsibilities:
- provide a sound family genetic/health history, if obtainable;
- obtain genetic evaluations of children, if indicated;
- assure that potentially adoptive parents are given full and accurate information about genetic findings; and
- inform prospective adoptive parents who have questions about genetics that genetic evaluation and counseling are available.

> **Uniform Adoption Act**
>
> (a) As early as practicable before a prospective adoptive parents accepts physical custody of a minor, a person placing the minor for adoption shall furnish to the prospective adoptive parent a written report containing all of the following information reasonably available from any person who has had legal or physical custody of the minor or who has provided medical, psychological, educational, or similar services to the minor:
>
> (1) a current medical and psychological history of the minor, including an account of the minor's prenatal care; medical condition at birth; any drug or medication taken by the minor's mother during pregnancy; any subsequent medical, psychological, or psychiatric examination and diagnosis; any physical, sexual, or emotional abuse suffered by the minor, and a record of any immunizations and health care received while in foster or other care;
>
> (2) relevant information concerning the medical and psychological history of the minor's genetic parents and relatives, including any known disease or hereditary predisposition to disease, any addiction to drugs or alcohol, the health of the minor's mother during her pregnancy, and the health of each parent at the minor's birth. . .
>
> [Uniform Adoption Act 1994, p. 26]

In sum, child welfare workers need to learn how to obtain genetic family histories because GFHs can help with a variety of tasks:
- support health promotion and disease prevention,
- aid in child welfare assessment and service planning,
- assist adult graduates of out-of-home care and adult adoptees with reproductive decision making, and
- protect against wrongful adoption and malpractice suits.

Many adoptive parents and adult adoptees may desire GFHs. A GFH is a health right for all children and in line with current trends towards providing fuller information to adult adoptees, graduates of out-of-home care, and adoptive parents.

Exercise 1. What Do You Think About Genetics?

Many observers are deeply concerned about the dangers of genetic knowledge and technology. Past abuses of genetic concepts by the eugenics movement in the United States and by Hitler's genocide of the Jews, people who were mentally retarded, homosexuals, and others on eugenic grounds contributed to a perception that an emphasis on genetics is socially dangerous. Currently, dangers include possible job and insurance discrimination on genetic grounds, a *new eugenics,* or pressures on women to terminate pregnancies of fetuses with genetic disorders, and resurgence of the old eugenics or pressures to sterilize people with genetic disorders and women who have given birth to alcohol- and drug-affected babies. Current pressures to reduce health care costs and welfare expenditures may support eugenic tendencies.

The history of sickle cell legislation in the United States offers a sobering lesson. Sickle cell disease is a serious inherited illness. In the United States, sickle cell disease occurs more often among African Americans than among other populations. The first mass carrier screening programs in the United States applied to sickle cell disease. These programs were stimulated by the 1972 Congressional enactment of the National Sickle Cell Anemia Control Act and the allocation of millions of dollars of federal funds. Unfortunately, poorly planned state programs had grave consequences for many African Americans. Some state programs failed to differentiate between carrier status and having the disease. Misinformation was presented in the medical literature, in educational brochures, and in the media. Identification of carrier status resulted in exclusion of many African Americans from participation in athletics, in exclusion from flight duty in the Armed Forces, in firing of African American flight attendants, and in needless increases in health and life insurance rates [Reilly 1977].

The first state mass genetic screening programs, some of which were mandatory, made insufficient provision of counseling to ensure that carriers understood the meaning of their status and reproductive risks. Many carriers needlessly worried about their health. Many did not understand the reproductive implications of carrier status. These and other problems associated with the first sickle cell screening programs led to controversy. Some African Americans argue that the sickle cell screening program diverted attention from the major causes of illness among African Americans [Gary 1974]. Sickle cell disease did not receive support for research and treatment proportionate to its incidence. Questions were raised about governmental emphasis on a program to identify carriers; some charged that sickle cell screening was a form of genocide.

The sickle cell experience illustrates several critical policy issues associated with genetic services and information: confidentiality, labeling and stigma, the values embedded in genetic policy, goals of genetic policy, allocation of social resources, possible governmental compulsion, and the risk of eugenicism.

These issues pertain to genetic services and information in child welfare. Important questions include:

- What is the purpose of obtaining a child's genetic family history? A genetic evaluation?
- To whom should information about a child's genetic status be given? When and under what circumstances?
- What impact will a genetic diagnosis have on a child's psychosocial development?
- How will others react to knowledge of a child's genetic status? What might be the effects on a child's life chances?
- What pressures might be applied to sexually active adolescents who have a genetic disorder or who carry a gene for a genetic disorder?

- Will biological parents of children with genetic disorders be pressured to have themselves sterilized? To obtain prenatal diagnosis? To terminate a pregnancy?
- What pressures might be applied to a pregnant teen or woman who abuses alcohol or other drugs? To women who have already given birth to a baby with fetal alcohol syndrome?

The exercise below is an opportunity to identify your opinions on genetic issues. We suggest that you answer each question and discuss the questions with members of your family, friends, and coworkers. We promise you will have some stimulating discussions!

What Do You Think About Genetics?

1. Have you had any formal instruction in human genetics and genetic services? If so, when?
2. Have you learned about human genetics, genetic disorders, and genetic services in other ways, such as the mass media or personal experience? What have been the primary sources of your learning?
3. What has been your personal experience with a genetic service? What was the service? Are you aware that many prenatal care facilities routinely do prenatal genetic screening of fetuses? What are your feelings about this?
4. If you have not received a genetic service, how do you think you would feel if you learned that you were a carrier of a gene for a serious genetic disorder? About learning that your unborn baby has a genetic disorder? About terminating a pregnancy for genetic reasons? About discovering that your school-age child has an inherited disorder?
5. What is your opinion about preventing women from becoming pregnant if they are or will be unable to care for their children because of uncontrolled mental illness, severe mental

retardation, substance abuse, or a history of child abuse? Do you think they should be sterilized? Should their pregnancies be terminated?

6. Allegations have been made that genetic services for people of color in the United States are genocidal. Do you agree or disagree with this idea? Why?

7. The federal government is funding research into the inheritance of psychiatric disorders. To what degree do you support this policy? What are your reasons for your opinion?

8. Predictions are that before the year 2005 it will be possible to identify all human genes. Do you think this knowledge is more likely to be helpful or harmful? What are the reasons for your opinion?

9. What do you think is the greatest benefit of obtaining a genetic family history for children who are or might become eligible for adoption? The greatest danger?

10. Do you think that parents and caregivers of children in your caseload might answer these questions differently than you? How might their answers be different? Why?

Exercise 2. Do You Want to Know About Faulty Genes?

1. All human beings have faulty genes that either *will* or *may* cause genetic disorders in themselves or their offspring. Answer the following questions for yourself.
   - Do you want to know about these genes?
   - Do you want others to know about them? Who? Why should they know? How might this information affect your relationships with them?
   - Are there certain individuals or corporations that you don't want to know about your genes? Who? Why?
2. Suppose your mother, or the mother of a loved one, had breast cancer.
   - Would you want testing for BRCA1 gene mutations, which account for a small percentage of breast cancer cases?
   - What about your adolescent daughter?
   - Suppose you or your loved one had a BRCA1 gene mutation. What might be the psychological effect? The effect on decisions to marry or to have children?
   - Some women are opting for radical prophylactic mastectomies (removal of healthy breasts to reduce the risk of cancer). Might you or your loved one do the same thing?
3. Mr. and Mrs. J. each carry the gene for cystic fibrosis, a serious, ultimately fatal disorder. At a reproductive center, eggs from Mrs. J. were fertilized in vitro by Mr. J's sperm. The embryos were examined genetically. Only embryos without the CF gene were transplanted to Mrs. J.'s uterus. Ms. J. became pregnant with twins, who were born healthy.
   - What do you think should be done with the embryos which have CF genes?
   - What are some implications for society of genetic selection of embryos for transplant? Should this practice be legal? Should it be outlawed?

Chapter 2
Selected Genetic Concepts

What Is a Gene?

Genes are involved in all human life processes. They affect all aspects of physical growth, development, functioning, and health. Genes are tiny messages responsible for all the biochemical processes of the human body. Each gene is like a word, or even a sentence, giving orders. Instead of letters, genes are composed of a biological code.

Genes are strung together on units called *chromosomes*. Humans normally have 23 pairs of chromosomes in each body cell, for a total of 46. Like identical twins, 22 pairs are matched. They carry the same genes, located in the same place. The 23rd pair is the sex chromosomes. The sex chromosomes are matched (XX) in women. They are unmatched (XY) in men.

There is one exception to the rule of 23 pairs of (46) chromosomes: egg and sperm cells. Each egg and sperm cell has only 23 chromosomes, one of each pair. When a sperm fertilizes an egg, the new cell ends up with 23 pairs. In this way, humans inherit half their chromosomes—and their genes—from their mothers, and half from their fathers.

Some people have likened genes to blueprints that direct the construction of a building. That image has some truth but is incomplete. Actually, constructing a building involves actions or processes. It requires tools, machines, people, communication, and coordination. People with specialized skills—like plumbers, electricians, carpenters, and masons—are needed. Workers have to communicate with each other. Supervisors coordinate different aspects of the work. The supervisors need to communicate with each other, the project director, and even the architect. Someone also has to be responsible for relations with the outside environment: ordering supplies, making sure they are delivered, paying the bills, maybe arranging for a loan if the contractor is running low on money, assuring compliance with the building code, advertising for tenants, and so on. Similarly, genes are like workers that bring the body's blueprint to life; they are involved in the coordinated and complex *processes* of construction, repair, maintenance, functioning, and environmental relations for the human body.

The Different Types of Genetic Disorders

Most of the 100,000 human genes are identical in all people. Some genes, however, have different forms. These variations contribute to the wonderful diversity that is the human family.

Sometimes a gene has a mistake in its "spelling," or code. Maybe a letter is out of place, or missing. Maybe there's an extra letter. Whatever the mistake, the result is that the gene doesn't do its job right. It may give the wrong directions, refuse to coordinate with others, ignore requests for supplies, order too many supplies, or send the supplies to the wrong place. It may just shut down or do just the opposite—work overtime.

Everyone has at least four or five faulty genes. Because genes come in pairs, the effects of these faulty genes may not be apparent. The effects are masked by their partners and may pass silently from generation to generation. Sometimes, however, a mistake in just one gene may cause a serious health problem. Some disorders occur when a person has only one copy of a faulty gene. Sometimes a person must have two copies of a faulty gene for a disorder to occur. Still other genetic problems result from the interaction of a single gene with environmental factors, or the interaction of several genes and the environment. Other genetic disorders are caused by mistakes in the number or structure of chromosomes. Sometimes environmental factors can interfere with normal genetic processes. Thus, there are four major types of genetic disorders: single gene, chromosomal, multifactorial, and environmentally induced.

Figure 1. Autosomal Dominant Inheritance

For an explanation of the symbols used in Figures 1–3, see Figure 6, page 59.

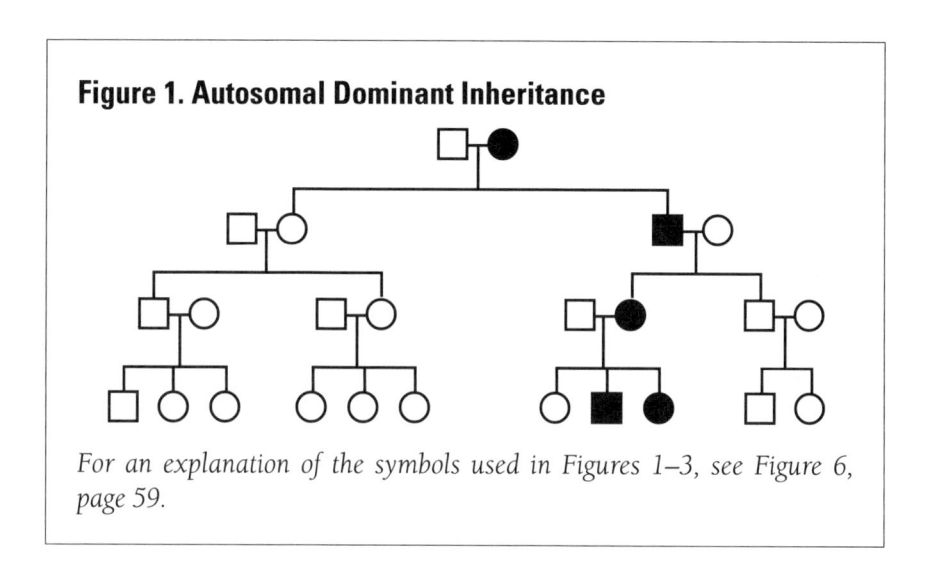

Single Gene Disorders

When a mistake in just one gene causes a disorder, the result is a *single gene disorder*. Genes differ in their strength. Some are stronger and dominate their partner. They are called *dominant* genes. Others are weaker than their partner. They are *recessive*. There are three major types of single gene disorders: dominant, recessive, and X-linked recessive.

Single copies of faulty dominant genes cause *dominant disorders*. Examples are Huntington's disease and neurofibromatosis. In dominant disorders, the gene—and its disorder—may pass from parent to child, as shown in Figure 1, above.

With each conception, chances are 50-50 that the dominant gene and the disorder will be inherited. Single gene disorders, however, may differ in severity from person to person. Sometimes, a parent is only mildly affected; the condition may not be recognized until after the birth of a more severely affected child. Similarly, a severely affected parent might have a mildly affected child. Thus, although it is possible to predict the chances that a child will inherit a dominant disorder, it is impossible to say whether the child will be severely or mildly affected. In some dominant disorders, individuals may carry the gene and not have any symptoms.

Figure 2. Autosomal Recessive Inheritance

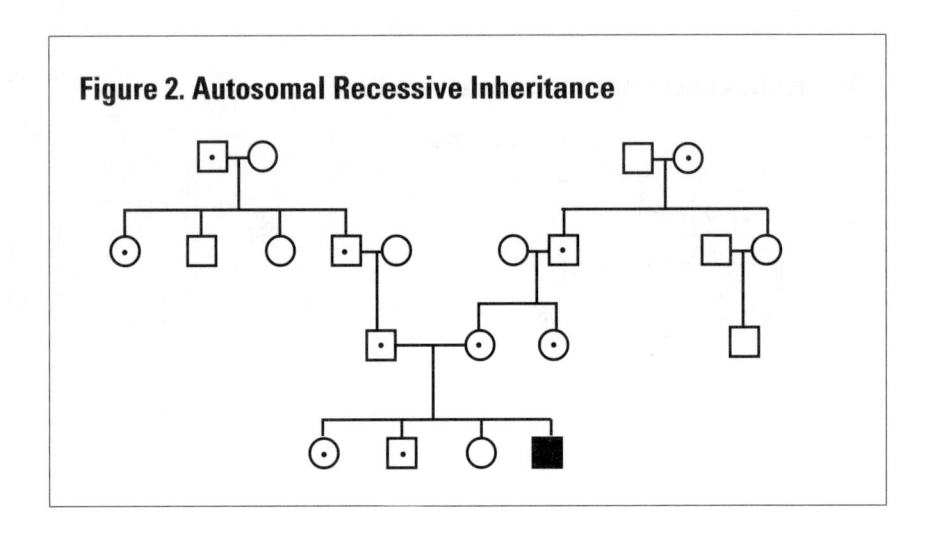

Recessive disorders occur when a person inherits two copies of a recessive gene, one from each parent. A recessive gene may pass silently from generation to generation, its presence being revealed only when a family member inherits two copies of the gene and develops the condition. When a mother and father each carry the same recessive gene, chances are 1 in 4 with each conception that a child will receive a copy from each parent and will develop the disorder, as seen in Figure 2, above.

Certain recessive disorders are more common in people from certain specific ethnic backgrounds. For example, cystic fibrosis is more common in people of Northern European background (Quick Reference #5, p. xiv). Recessive disorders are also more common when parents are blood relatives, as when cousins marry or in cases of incest. Examples of recessive disorders are cystic fibrosis, sickle cell disease, and Tay-Sachs disease.

Another type of single gene disorder is *X-linked recessive*. These occur mainly in males. Remember that males have unmatched (XY) sex chromosomes. If a recessive gene is carried on a male's X chromosome, it doesn't have a stronger, dominant partner to stop its action. If a female carries a faulty gene on one of her X chromosomes, her second X chromosome will carry a strong partner gene that will overpower the faulty recessive gene. (See Figure 3.)

Figure 3. X-Linked Recessive Inheritance

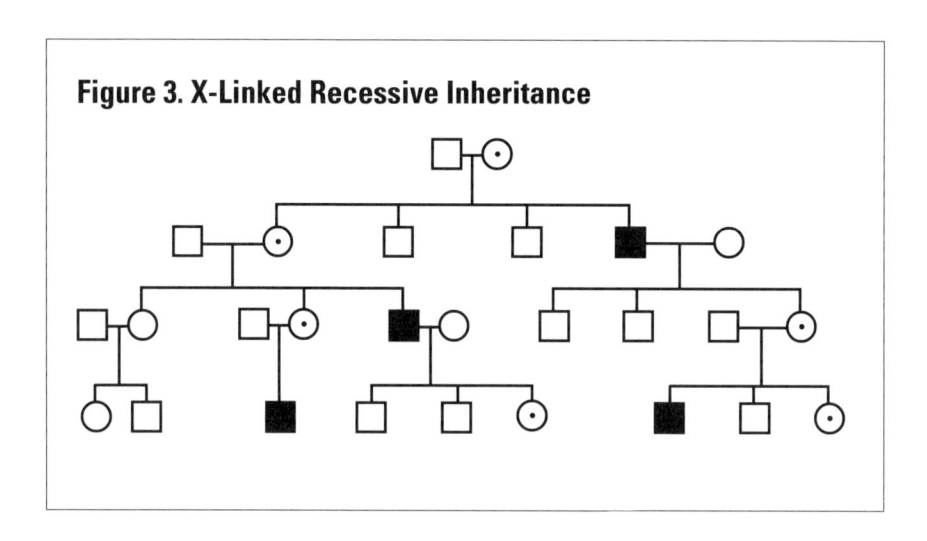

The gene for X-linked recessive disorders is transmitted from an unaffected mother to an affected son. With each conception of a male, chances are 50-50 that a carrier mother will pass on the X-chromosome that carries the faulty gene. Similarly, there is a 50-50 chance that each female conceived will inherit the gene. Although she may not have the disorder, she could, like her mother, pass it on to her sons. Hemophilia is a relatively common X-linked recessive disorder.

Chromosome Disorders

Chromosome disorders involve a mistake in the number of chromosomes or their structure. Any chromosome can be affected, including a sex chromosome. Chromosome disorders are generally serious and can result in miscarriages, birth defects, and mental retardation. Down syndrome, which used to be referred to as *mongolism,* is a fairly common chromosome disorder caused by an extra chromosome 21.

Usually, the faulty chromosome is created when a mistake occurs in cell division of sperm, eggs, or the fertilized egg. For that reason, most chromosome disorders are not inherited and don't run in families. Exceptions occur, however. Geneticists diagnose chromosome disorders by using a special microscope to look at the chromosomes in a sample of a person's blood or skin.

Multifactorial Conditions

Many of our traits result from gene-environment interaction. Height and weight are everyday examples. Skin color is a multifactorial trait that is affected by both internal and external environments—illness, the sun, embarrassment, and even eating too many carrots!

Many disorders, including major psychiatric illnesses, are known or suspected of being caused by gene-environment interactions, or having *multifactorial inheritance*. Sometimes, the environmental factor is known, as in diabetes, a disorder of sugar metabolism, or some allergies. Sometimes, the environmental factors are not known, or are only suspected.

Birth defects are often multifactorial. Many common diseases of adulthood, such as coronary artery disease and hypertension, are multifactorial. Major psychiatric illnesses may be caused by the interaction of genetic and environmental factors.

Unlike single gene disorders, multifactorial disorders have no sharply defined inheritance patterns. Nonetheless, they clearly run in families. Experts agree that genes play a role; someone who has a first-degree relative with a multifactorial condition is more likely than unrelated individuals to have affected offspring.

When the environmental factors are unknown, little can be done to prevent a multifactorial condition. A lot can be done when the environmental factors are known, however. For example, a person at risk for high blood pressure can use less salt or watch his or her weight. The opportunity to prevent some multifactorial conditions, or to lessen their severity, is one reason why genetic family histories are so important for children who are in out-of-home care or are being adopted.

Environmentally Induced Conditions

Some birth defects and health problems appear to be entirely caused by harmful environmental agents (see Quick Reference #4, pp. x–xiii). Examples are black lung disease in miners or fetal alcohol syndrome in newborns.

Future research may reveal that some conditions, which today appear to be caused by environmental factors, are in fact multifactorial. For example, cigarette smoking causes most lung cancer. Not all smokers develop lung cancer, however. It is likely that the difference between those who do and those who don't become ill may be a genetic predisposition.

Birth defects caused by prenatal exposure to harmful environmental agents, such as alcohol, are a problem in child welfare. In addition to recreational drugs, some prescribed medications may injure the developing baby. An example is lithium, which is used to treat bipolar disorder (sometimes called manic depression). Certain viral infections, such as rubella (German measles), are also dangerous to the fetus if they occur during pregnancy. Exposure to X-rays is also damaging. (See Quick Reference #4, p. xiii.)

Another category of potentially harmful agents is chronic illness. Women with some chronic illnesses are more likely than healthy women to have babies with birth defects. Examples are diabetes and phenylketonuria, also known as PKU. Babies born to women with HIV/AIDS usually do not have birth defects, even though they can be born HIV-infected.

Sometimes, the effects of the environmental agent don't show up at birth but appear later. This is sometimes the case with children with substance-abusing biological mothers. The child may seem okay during infancy and as a toddler, but problems of poor concentration, hyperactivity, or learning deficits, for example, may show up in school.

Doctors often have a hard time diagnosing the cause of a birth defect. Just as a headache can have different causes in different people, or in the same person at different times, the same birth defect can result from different causes in different babies. For example, mental retardation can be caused by multifactorial inheritance, single gene disorders, chromosomal problems, prenatal exposure to alcohol, premature birth, or lead poisoning. Medical geneticists are physicians who are specially trained to diagnose birth defects.

Knowing the cause can be extremely important to the affected person and biological family members. If a birth defect is genetic, the affected individual and other family members may be at risk for having offspring with the same problem. If an environmental agent caused the defect, future offspring are at no special risk.

Chapter 3

Genetic Services

Genetic services encompass screening, diagnostic evaluations, genetic counseling, and treatment. Genetic service capabilities are expanding rapidly, and a service that is not available today may be available tomorrow.

If you ever wonder if a specific service is available, help is just a telephone away. A genetic counselor at your nearest genetics center will be happy to answer your questions. For information about how to locate a genetics center, see Quick Reference #2, p. viii.

Genetic Screening and Testing

Four types of genetic screening and testing are available: carrier, presymptomatic, prenatal, newborn.

Carrier screening identifies individuals who are carriers—usually healthy individuals who have faulty gene mutations that could cause specific genetic disorders in their children. Carrier screening is possible for only some single gene conditions, including cystic fibrosis, sickle cell disease, and Tay-Sachs, but the number of single gene conditions for which carrier screening is available increases almost daily.

Carrier screening is recommended for members of families with known histories of genetic disorders, and for members of ethnic groups known to have higher than average incidences of genes for specific genetic disorders. (See Quick Reference #5, p. xiv.) In the future, it may be possible to identify carriers for conditions that are associated with the interaction of two or more specific genes.

Presymptomatic screening is a form of carrier screening. It identifies individuals who carry the gene for a specific, later onset disorder—one that appears after birth, for example—and are at increased risk to develop the condition. For instance, hereditary breast cancer occurs in a few families. Features of hereditary breast cancer include diagnosis before age 50, multiple affected family members, and breast cancer in more than one breast or at multiple sites within one breast.

The predisposition for hereditary breast cancer is autosomal dominant—that is, only one mutated copy of the gene is needed; the gene mutation can be passed from parent to child. It is now possible to test women for mutations in the genes that can predispose to hereditary breast cancer. A woman who has a mutation in one of these genes is at significant increased risk to develop breast cancer in her lifetime. Presymptomatic screening is currently available for only a few conditions. It, too, is likely to become available for more and more conditions.

Prenatal screening identifies pregnant women who may be carrying a baby with a birth defect. One screening technique is *sonography*, a way of viewing the fetus. Another is laboratory testing of a sample of the mother's blood to determine the level of a particular biochemical associated with birth defects. If screening suggests that the baby may have a birth defect, the mother is usually referred to a clinical genetics center for further diagnostic study and genetic counseling.

Newborn screening identifies the possible presence of certain serious but treatable genetic diseases in newborns. Screening is conducted within a day or two of birth, before symptoms appear. There are some dramatic newborn screening success stories. For example, new cases of mental retardation caused by several inherited metabolic diseases have almost been eliminated due to newborn screening and immediately placing affected newborns on special diets.

Diagnostic Evaluations

There are two major types of diagnostic evaluations. One is prenatal diagnosis, or evaluation of a fetus before birth. The other is assessment of infants, children, adolescents, and adults who may have a genetic disorder.

Clinical geneticists—doctors with specialized training in diagnosing and treating genetic disorders and who are certified by the American Board of Human Genetics—make genetic diagnoses.

A genetic diagnosis begins with a review of medical records and the family genetic history. The process includes a physical examination, laboratory tests, and biochemical tests. It is actually possible in the laboratory to look at a person's genes and chromosomes and find out if he or she has a specific gene or a faulty chromosome.

Physical examination of a fetus is not possible, so other approaches are available for prenatal diagnosis. Sonography makes it possible to look at the fetus to see if it has a birth defect. Other techniques use samples of the mother's blood or fetal cells from the developing placenta or from the fluid in the sac that carries and protects the infant. Although it seldom happens, these techniques can result in miscarriage. Genetic counselors help parents decide whether they want prenatal testing by explaining the techniques and their risks, benefits, and limitations. The list of disorders that can be diagnosed before birth is growing rapidly.

Genetic Counseling

Genetic counseling is a core genetic service. Genetic counseling is available to carriers, pregnant couples, and individuals and families affected by genetic disorders. Carriers often wonder about what would happen if they married another carrier, about whether to have children, and about their reproductive options.

Genetic counseling is also important for people who learn that their unborn baby has a birth defect or genetic disease. They may benefit from information about the condition and from thinking about the impact upon the family of having a child with a genetic disorder. Genetic counselors provide information, emotional support, and counseling to parents for whom termination of pregnancy for genetic reasons is an option. Such a decision is usually painful, even tormenting.

Clinical geneticists, counselors with master's degrees in genetic counseling, and other health professionals—including social workers—with sufficient training and experience provide genetic counseling, which may include the following responsibilities:
- educating clients concerning the cause, prognosis, and treatment of a genetic disorder;
- discussing the inheritance pattern and chances that the disorder will occur in other family members;
- reviewing reproductive options;
- assisting in decision making;
- helping families cope with the genetic disorder; and
- offering emotional support.

Optimally, genetic counseling accompanies all genetic services. Unfortunately, this is not always the case. When counseling is not provided, people may misunderstand the genetic information they receive. For example, many people do not understand the difference between being a carrier and being affected by a genetic disorder. People who learn that they are carriers may be devastated, believing that they have a fatal genetic disorder.

Genetic counselors are an important resource for you. They can answer questions about whether a pregnant woman or child should be seen at a genetics center. If a child has a genetic condition, genetic counselors can provide information about the disorder, its treatment, and its prognosis.

Genetic counselors also know a lot about the psychosocial aspects of genetic disorders. They know about local resources, including peer support groups. Most will also be delighted to arrange for in-service training for child welfare agency staff.

Chapter 4
Referrals to Genetic Services

Criteria for Genetic Referrals

Who should be referred for genetic services? Specific criteria are given in Quick Reference #1, p. vii. As a child welfare worker, you are most likely to refer infants, children, or adolescents in your caseload who meet the referral criteria, or preadoptive and adoptive parents who have questions about the implications of a child's genetic family history. From time to time, you may want to refer clients with reproductive concerns—for example, a biological mother who has had multiple miscarriages or an adolescent who wonders if he or she carries the gene for a genetic disorder that runs in his or her family.

> Camille, 17, and her two older brothers entered foster care when they were preschoolers, after their father, who is now incarcerated, killed their mother. Both her brothers developed muscular dystrophy. Alex died when he was 18. Andrew, 19, now uses a wheelchair and is likely to live only for another year or two. Camille wonders if she carries the gene for muscular dystrophy and if she can have healthy children.

Contacting the Genetic Center

What if you are not sure whether a child should be referred to a genetics center? Help is only a telephone call away. Call the nearest clinical genetics center. Suggestions for locating genetic services are given in Quick Reference #2, p. viii.

When you telephone the genetic service, ask to speak to a genetic counselor. The counselor will answer your questions and help you decide whether the referral is appropriate. The counselor will also tell you how to make an appointment, the information that should be provided, what the client can expect, and information about health insurance coverage. If Medicaid or other health insurance in your state refuses to reimburse for the service, the genetic counselor can help you to advocate for reimbursement by documenting the need.

Signed consent for certain medical procedures and for release of records is required. When children are involved, the person or agency legally responsible for the child must give written consent. Be sure to arrange for the legally authorized person to come to the genetics appointment. If that is not possible, ask the genetics counselor to send you the necessary forms ahead of time. Obtain the needed signature before the appointment.

Telling the Individual and Family About the Referral

It is important to plan how you will tell the people involved about the genetic services referral. Planning is necessary, because people may worry about what the geneticist might discover. Simply put, they may be afraid the geneticist will give them bad news.

A second reason for planning how to recommend the referral is that genetics touches on vital, sensitive areas, such as sexuality, being different, whether to have children, and possible early death. The person may come from a family that is keeping secrets about stigmatized disorders, such as relatives' mental illness or mental retardation. The family may also be keeping incest a secret. For these reasons, a genetic referral may trigger anxiety and resistance. The people involved may not want to discuss genetic issues with you. They may be unwilling to accept your recommendation to obtain a genetic service.

It is particularly important to prepare your presentation if you are working with an involuntary client. Anger, fear, and suspicion are common reactions of involuntary clients to child welfare workers. The person may be hostile, unwilling to receive services, resentful, and defensive. The person may break an appointment with you. If she does see you, the person may talk little, give short answers, question you and, possibly lie.

When talking with parents or other biological relatives, emphasize that the genetic referral will benefit the child, that the goal is to obtain medical information that will help doctors to provide good medical care to the child. Recognize possible anxiety by commenting that many people feel uncomfortable talking about family health. Stress that the geneticist will respect their privacy. State who should have the information and why. Mention the need for informed consent for release of information. Encourage people to express their concerns about the genetics referral. Empathize. Acknowledge their love for the child and their desire to do what is best for him or her.

Planning your presentation is necessary too when working with clients of diverse cultural backgrounds. Their health beliefs and practices may differ from those of Western medicine. Talking about a child's health problem may also be taboo. Culture and genetics are discussed in Chapter 13.

If the legally responsible person refuses to consent to a recommended genetic evaluation, ask a medical geneticist about the possible consequences to the child. What are the chances that a serious condition will be untreated because it is not recognized? What are the likely consequences if the condition is not treated? Is there a possible threat to the child's functioning, even his or her life? After obtaining the geneticist's opinion, talk with your supervisor about whether the refusal is medical neglect and what actions, if any, you should take. In some instances, you or your supervisor may want to consult a lawyer.

Planning your presentation is also vital when referring children or adolescents for genetic evaluation. What you tell and how depends on the reason for the referral and the child's age, cognitive development, emotional health, understanding of the problem, and experience with medical settings. It is important to use the child's words for the problem. Explain the referral in positive terms, such as wanting to find out the reason for the problem and what can be done to make things easier. It is important to prepare children for what will happen, including taking off their clothes, physical examination, being stuck with a needle, or having their picture taken.

Sometimes diagnoses have positive emotional effects. Chances are that the child or adolescent knew there was a problem. They may have wondered, "What is wrong with me?" The diagnosis gives them an answer and may let them know what can be done. Helping the client to meet other people with the same condition can be quite helpful. The client may feel less alone.

And, sometimes, the diagnosis is devastating.

> Pablo G., a 16-year-old living in a group home, learned that he had Klinefelter syndrome, a condition that affects males only. Adolescents and men with Klinefelter are often unusually tall. They are also infertile. Thus, Pablo learned that he could never have biological children. He became depressed and suicidal. The worker referred him for counseling and also taught him how to contact other people with Klinefelter syndrome through the Internet.

Telling adolescents and young adults about carrier screening can be ticklish. They may not know about the genetic disorder that runs in their biological family or their ethnic group. If they know about it, they may not understand its implications for themselves and their offspring, they may have mistaken ideas, or they may be fearful of the results. Talking about their biological families may bring to the surface feelings of abandonment, loss, grief, and rage. Thus, the topic needs to be sensitively introduced.

Often the teen or young adult who is at genetic risk will express or hint at a genetic concern. The information that carrier screening is available can be presented in the context of the stated concerns. Others may deny or minimize genetic issues. One way to introduce the topic is to present it as a normal concern:

> Sometimes people who hope to have children worry that there is a health problem that runs in their biological families that they could give to their children. What about you? Have you sometimes worried about this?

Depending on the condition, you may be able to provide brochures about the condition and carrier screening. Do not try to give technical genetic information yourself. Do not make promises about the questions genetic counselors can answer. Unless you are very, very sure of what the genetic counselor will be able to do, be uncertain: "The genetic counselor *may* be able to tell you…." Stress that the genetic counselor will be able to provide information that can be used in deciding whether to be screened for carrier status.

When preadoptive or adoptive parents have questions about a child's genetic condition or genetic family history, they should be referred to a genetic counselor if financially feasible. The parents may hope that a genetic counselor will answer all their questions and calm all their anxieties. That is not the case. For example, a genetic counselor will usually not be able to predict how sick a child with a genetic disease will be—that is simply not possible at the present time. One child with cystic fibrosis may be so sick that she dies at age 6 months; in another, the disease may be so mild that it is not recognized until late adolescence. Similarly, it is impossible at this time to predict with certainty whether a child will inherit a mother's schizophrenia or other multifactorial disorders.

Even though genetic counselors may not be able to answer all preadoptive and adoptive parents' questions about a child at genetic risk, they can provide useful information and answer *some* questions. In general, you should refer parents to a genetic counselor rather than try to answer people's genetic questions yourself. You might give inaccurate or misleading information. Any genetic information should be given in writing and documented. Fortunately, most genetic centers routinely provide written summaries. Be sure the document is placed with other health records.

What Information Should Be Provided to the Geneticist?

The genetic family history is vital. Optimally, the parents or other biological family members who are knowledgeable about both the mother's and father's genetic family histories will come to the appointment so that a genetics professional can obtain the genetic family history.

It is likely, however, that you will need to provide the history that you and other workers have obtained at different points in the youngster's time in the child welfare system. If you are referring for carrier screening, the history is the only information you will need to bring. The history is also sufficient when you are referring for genetic counseling regarding a single gene disorder with a confirmed diagnosis.

Additional information should be provided if you are referring for a genetic evaluation or counseling for a multifactorial condition. When you call the genetics center, someone will tell you what information to bring. Possibilities include records of prenatal care, birth, newborn nursery, and other medical records. The genetics center may request reports of any developmental evaluations. In some instances, records of relatives' affected by the condition of concern may be useful if they can be obtained. For example, bipolar disorder in children is sometimes misdiagnosed as ADHD. In this case, information that a biological relative had bipolar disorder can help to point to the correct diagnosis. When making a genetic referral, you can refresh your information about the information needed by reviewing Quick Reference #3, p. ix.

What Will Happen to a Child at a Genetics Evaluation?

During the evaluation, the clinical geneticist will review the medical and family history information. The child's clothes will be removed so that the geneticist can perform a careful physical examination. The physical examination may be more thorough than a routine physical examination. The geneticist may, for example, measure a child's head size, finger length, distance between the eyes, etc. The geneticist may also want to photograph the child to document his or her physical features and to use as a baseline to watch changes over time. Signed consent to photograph, separate from the consent to medical procedures, will be needed.

The geneticist may want samples of blood to conduct laboratory studies, depending on the genetic disorder of concern. The blood may be taken by the geneticist, a genetics center nurse, or another department within the hospital. Obviously, some children are afraid of being stuck by a needle. They may need to be reassured while the blood is being taken, and comforted afterwards.

The geneticist may also want the child to be seen by other health professionals. For example, a child with visual problems or unusual appearing eyes should be seen by an eye doctor; a child with weak muscles should be seen by a neurologist. Appointments with other doctors may be scheduled on the same day as the genetics visit. The result may be a long and tiring day. The child may need to sit in a waiting room for periods of time. Bringing toys, games, or books to help pass the time is recommended. Buying lunch and snacks may be necessary, or you may bring your own. It is also possible that the other appointments will be scheduled for another day, making it necessary to return to the medical center one or more times.

After the diagnosis, the genetic counselor or medical geneticist will meet with the appropriate people. This may include the biological parents, foster parents or other caretakers, and the child welfare worker. Whether adolescents should be included will depend on their preferences and their intellectual, emotional, and psychosocial functioning. Whether potential adoptive parents should be included will depend on the stage of the adoption process.

The genetics team will present medical information about the disorder, its cause, course, prognosis, and available treatment, if any. You should request a written report explaining the diagnosis and recommended follow-up for the agency's records, the person's doctor or health care facility, and caretaker. If available, the counselor will give you brochures about the condition and information on support groups, names and addresses of information sources, or local resources.

Paying for Genetic Services

The cost of genetic services varies regionally and depends on the services provided. Whether Medicaid or other insurance coverage is available varies by service, state, and insurer. Health maintenance organizations also vary in coverage. Whether the client will be eligible for Supplemental

Security Income will also vary by the specific disorder and degree of disability.

Services of outreach genetics clinics are often provided at a reduced charge. Sliding fee scales may be used for indigent families. Health care services and delivery systems are changing rapidly, however. Again, the genetic counselor should be able to answer your questions about costs and coverage in your state. The genetic counselor can also help you obtain documentation if you need to advocate for coverage that was denied.

Chapter 5
Conducting the History-Taking Interview

Optimally, you will obtain a child's genetic family history by scheduling interviews with informed members of both the maternal and paternal families, solely for the purpose of obtaining the history. Often that will not be possible. In that case, you will need to be alert to opportunities to obtain family history information even when you are focusing on something else.

> You mentioned that your grandmother died of a heart problem. How old was she when she died? Have other members of your family also had heart problems?

Whether you obtain genetic family information in a special interview or obtain it during the course of other interviews, the principles discussed in this chapter apply.

Your approach to taking a family health/genetic history will differ according to the nature of your relationship with the person who is providing the history. For example, if a child is in out-of-home care, a biological parent may be hostile toward you. A grandmother providing kinship care may or may not see you as interested and caring. Your role is also a factor. Are you a protective services worker investigating charges of neglect and abuse? Are you an adoption worker who has a warm ongoing relationship with a biological mother who is relinquishing her child for adoption? Preparatory "tuning-in" is necessary to prepare you for the contact with the family member.

Preparatory Tuning In

The following steps can help you to prepare for the interview:
- Review the information you have about the child. Does the information suggest that the child may have a chronic illness, developmental disability, or handicapping condition, or that the child was exposed prenatally to harmful environmental agents, such as alcohol? Are there any medical terms in the child's records that you don't understand? Is there a health problem that seems to run in the family? Should you educate yourself about a particular problem before taking the history?
- Empathically think about the encounter between yourself and the person who will be giving you the family health history. How is the person likely to perceive you? How is the person likely to feel about meeting with you and about telling you private family information?
- What are some possible barriers to your ability to engage this person? How does the person probably perceive the agency? What is your role within the agency? Are you of the same or different gender, the same or different race, or the same or different ethnicity? Are there marked differences in your ages? Are there class differences or cultural differences?
- What can you do to reduce any potential barriers?
- How do you feel about meeting with this person?
- Does the person speak English? If not, do you need an interpreter?
- What are some points of connection between you and the other person that you can use to create a positive relationship? For example, can you comment on how well the child has done in school, the child's good looks, or special talents? What similarities between you and the person can you use to understand and engage the person?
- Might the person have folk beliefs about the causes of chronic illnesses and disabilities in children that differ from the explanations of Western medicine? How can you respect those beliefs while asking for the family health history?

The History-Taking Interview

Beginnings are important in interviews. A good beginning can get you off to a good start. A poor beginning can alienate the other person and doom the interview. Here are some tips for a good beginning:
- In general, avoid the use of the person's first name. Address the person by title—Mr., Mrs., or Ms.—unless the person asks you to use another form of address.
- Observe courtesies and civilities, such as introducing yourself, appreciating the person's agreeing to talk with you, offering to hang up a person's coat (if she is coming to your office), making some small talk. Remember that different cultures have different courtesy behaviors.
- If you are interviewing a family, ask who will be the spokesperson. In some families from other cultures, for example, it may be inappropriate for an outsider to speak to a woman or to a child. Observe the family's cultural rules, even if you disagree with them.
- To facilitate engaging the person or family, try to begin the interaction with a positive remark that will connect you and the person, no matter how slight the connection. For example, you may want to make a remark to the person such as, "I like that color blouse you are wearing. I have a blouse in just the same color" or "I see that you were born in July. My son was born in July." You might want to comment on the child's strengths: "Todd is such a polite child" or "I understand that Jamal is doing well at school."
- If the person is an immigrant, ask how long he or she has been in the United States. Recent immigrants may be less aware of American culture than those who have been here for several years. Ask the person to let you know if he doesn't understand what you say. Speak more slowly than usual. Be aware that the person may come from a culture in which beliefs about health, health problems, health care, and inheritance are different those of American culture. Tell the person that you are not familiar with the customs of his or her culture. Ask the person to be your teacher and to tell you if you ask about something that it would be impolite to discuss within his or her culture.

- Explain the purpose of the interview and that the family genetic history is important for the child's health and well-being. Modify your explanation, if need be, so that it is congruent with the person's culture.
- Explain that you will be taking notes, that this is necessary so you are sure to get the information down correctly and because you do not want to forget anything. Ask if this is okay with the person. Drawing a diagram of the family history (see Chapter 7) is a helpful way of involving the person in the process. Offer to let the person look at your notes or to give him or her a copy of your notes or your report.
- Give a rationale for the questions to be asked.

Asking about family health histories requires tact and sensitivity. Before beginning, explain to the person that the information is routinely obtained, why it is important, and how it will be used. Note that the information is confidential, and state whether and to whom it will be given—for example, the child's doctor or a geneticist. Acknowledge that sharing one's family health histories can sometimes be hard to do.

Remember these tips for interviewing involuntary or reluctant clients:
- State who you are.
- Avoid using the person's first name unless asked or given permission to do so.
- Be respectful.
- Do not show anger toward the person.
- Accept the person for who he or she is.
- Do not belittle the person.
- Be supportive.
- Begin where the person is; listen to his or her ideas and perceptions.
- Express appropriate empathy: "I hear your frustration."
- Explain why you want genetic family history information, including how the child will benefit.
- Explore the person's view of your wanting a family genetic history.
- Remember that the person's anger or hostility toward you is not personal but is directed toward your role and what you represent.
- After the interview is ended, be sure to thank the person for his or her time and cooperation.

Exercise #3. Your Family Genetic History

Diagram your own family genetic history. What was it like for you to do this? Did you have any feelings of anxiety, sadness, or shame? How would you feel if you had to share this history with a stranger? What could another person do to make you feel more comfortable about sharing your genetic family history?

Chapter 6
Obtaining the Genetic Family History

The genetic family history (GFH) should include information on the health and medical history of the child's living and deceased relatives, including full and half siblings, parents, aunts, uncles, cousins, and grandparents, if obtainable.

You can use several approaches to obtain the family's health and genetic history. One is to ask a few open-ended questions, such as:
- "How is your family's health?"
- "Tell me about your mother's health."

You can then ask more focused questions:
- "Has any ailment affected more than one member of your family?"
- "When did your grandmother die? How old was she? What did she die of? Did other members of your family have the same illness as your grandmother?"

The information you obtain can be written down. It is important, however, to keep the information in one place rather than buried in different locations in the child's ongoing record, where it might be overlooked. If a child's record does not contain a separate section for a health history, we suggest you create one. New information should be entered on the summary document that will be seen by the child's physician or physicians. That is, you may need to note the information more than once, depending upon how your agency's records are set up.

The broad, open-ended approach is the easiest and probably more comfortable for you and the person to whom you are talking. Important information may be forgotten or overlooked, however, when using an informal approach. The best practice is to devote an entire interview to obtaining the family health history from people who are informed about both the maternal and paternal histories and who can contact other relatives to obtain further information if needed.

Obstacles to Obtaining Genetic Family Histories

For several reasons, GFH information is often difficult, even impossible, to obtain for many children involved with child welfare services. One, of course, is abandonment—a child's parents may be unknown. Another is that the parent or other family members may know little, if anything, about the other parent's family. The father may not be unknown or unavailable. People may hold some things secret out of shame or embarrassment. If something is painful, a person may deny it occurred or may suppress the memory altogether. For example, it may be "forgotten" that a parent was alcoholic or committed suicide.

Not only is a GFH often hard to obtain, you may not have the luxury of sitting down with a family member to systematically ask about the information. You may be going from crisis to crisis. You may be pressed for time because your caseload is too heavy. You may be under a deadline to prepare documentation for a court hearing.

Even though you face several obstacles to obtaining a client's GFH, we hope we have persuaded you to make a good faith effort to obtain as much information as possible. Chances are that several workers will obtain bits and pieces of a family history at different times during a child's welfare career. Recording the information in accessible locations, therefore, as described in the next chapter, is essential.

What Do You Already Know?

A good way to start recording a GFH is to ask yourself what you already know. Chances are good that you know something about the child's ethnic background. Remember that members of certain ethnic groups are more likely to have the gene for or be affected by certain inherited conditions.

Record whatever ethnic information you have about the child's parents and grandparents.

In addition to possibly knowing the client's ethnicity, you may be informed in other areas. For example, you may know that the mother was an alcoholic who drank heavily during pregnancy. You may know that she was unable to care for her children because she was in a psychiatric hospital. You may know that the mother and father's parenting abilities are limited because both are mentally retarded. You may know that a teen was repeatedly molested by her biological father and that he may be father of her child. All this information belongs in a GFH. Be sure to indicate the source of information and whether it is documented or alleged. The source of the documentation or allegation should be recorded.

What Written Information Can You Obtain?

Written records often contain a wealth of information. They may even include a previously obtained GFH! The GFH may be buried in a record, however. For example, physicians often take GFHs during diagnostic work-ups and include them in chart notes. The GFH may not be summarized in medical reports, however. Thus, you may want to request copies of full medical records rather than summary reports.

Helpful records include:
- prenatal care records;
- birth records;
- a child's other medical records;
- school records;
- records of a child's evaluations or treatment for developmental delay, learning problems, psychiatric symptoms, etc.;
- medical records of parents and other family members; and
- death certificates of deceased family members.

Some Basic Questions to Ask

Following are some basic questions to ask. Optimally, you will ask these questions of informed biological family members from both the mother's and father's families. You can also ask these questions of written records

that you have obtained. If the answer to any of these is "Yes," consider a genetic services referral.
- On either side of the family, is there anyone with mental retardation, learning disabilities, or developmental delay?
- On either side of the family, is there anyone born with a birth defect, such as missing fingers or a heart problem?
- Has anyone in the family lost three or more pregnancies?
- Have any family members, children or any adults, died at a young age for reasons other than accident or injury?
- Has anyone in the family been chronically ill since childhood. Has anyone been on a special diet since childhood?
- Did anyone in the family become blind, deaf, or need a wheelchair at a young age?
- Has anyone in the family been on medication for a long time or hospitalized frequently?
- Is there any condition in the family that anyone has worried or wondered about because it seemed to be inherited?

For pregnancy history:
- Were there any problems during the pregnancy, such as bleeding, cramping, infections, or maternal illness?
- Did the mother use any medications, drugs, or use alcohol during the pregnancy?
- Was the pregnancy full term? Were there any complications during delivery?

Another approach is to use a longer, detailed, structured format. An example is given in Appendix B. Another is to diagram the information, as described in the next chapter.

Chapter 7
Recording the Information

The genetic family history (GFH) should be recorded in at least one accessible location, not scattered throughout a child's record. It can be recorded in different ways. Your agency may already have a form you are required to use. Model forms have also been developed. Unfortunately, most model forms that we have seen are too complicated for use by busy child welfare workers facing the GFH obstacles mentioned in Chapter 6. *The important thing is that all the GFH information be recorded in the same location in the child's record and that it be available to both health care providers and the child's current and future workers.*

In this chapter, we will present the format developed by the Maryland Department of Human Resources for inclusion on its health passport for children in out-of-home care, and we will describe how to construct a "pedigree," or graph, of a genetic family history.

The Maryland Health Passport

The Maryland Department of Human Resources has developed a one-page health passport for children in out-of-home care throughout the state (Figures 4 and 5). The passport includes space for the family history on the first page, including space the prenatal and birth history, immunizations, sexual information, and family information. The reverse side (Figure 5) provides instructions and lists 20 major health problems, each of which (except for HIV) may have genetic causes and may warrant a genetic services referral.

Figure 4. Maryland Health Passport: Child's Health History

FORM 631-B	Health Passpost **CHILD'S HEALTH HISTORY** (See instructions on reverse)	☐ ORIGINAL ☐ UPDATE (Complete 1, 2, 6, plus new information)
1. CHILD'S NAME		2. DATE FORM COMPLETED
3. BIRTH DATE	4. SEX	5. LDSS	6. WORKER NAME & ID#	7. TELEPHONE

I. PRENATAL - BIRTH

CHILDREN UNDER 5 YEARS OLD

1. PRENATAL CARE PROVIDED TO MOTHER? ☐ YES ☐ NO	2. HOSPITAL CHILD BORN IN	ADDRESS	ZIP
3. GESTATION ☐ PRE TERM ☐ SINGLE BIRTH ☐ FULL TERM ☐ MULTIPLE BIRTH ☐ POST TERM	4. DELIVERY ☐ NORMAL ☐ OTHER (specify) ☐ UNKNOWN	5. COMPLICATIONS DURING NEWBORN PERIOD ☐ CONVULSIONS ☐ JAUNDICE ☐ FEEDING PROBLEMS ☐ RED BLOOD COUNT (high/low) ☐ INFECTIONS ☐ INTENSIVE CARE NURSERY	☐ RESPIRATORY ☐ OTHER (specify below) ☐ UNKNOWN

ALL CHILDREN

| 6. MOTHER'S USE WHILE PREGNANT
☐ ALCOHOL ☐ OTHER DRUGS (specify)
☐ TOBACCO ☐ NONE
☐ MEDICATIONS (specify) ☐ UNKNOWN | 7. BIRTH DEFECTS | 8. CHILD DISEASES
☐ CHICKEN POX
☐ OTHER (specify)
☐ UNKNOWN | 9. ARE CHILD'S PARENTS BLOOD RELATIVES?
☐ YES
☐ NO
☐ UNKNOWN |

II. HOSPITALIZATIONS

DATES	REASON/DIAGNOSIS	HOSPITAL (Name and Address)

III. IMMUNIZATIONS

DOSE NUMBER	VACCINE TYPE (enter date immunized)						
	DPT	DT(PED)	POLIO	Td	HIB	HEP-B	MMR
1st DOSE							
2nd DOSE							
3rd DOSE							
4th DOSE							
5th DOSE							

IV. SEXUAL INFORMATION

A. SEXUALLY TRANSMITTED DISEASES? ☐ YES ☐ NO	B. SEXUALLY ACTIVE? ☐ YES ☐ UNK ☐ NO	C. BIRTH CONTROL METHOD?	D. # OF PREGNANCIES	E. LIVING CHILDREN

Figure 4. Maryland Health Passport: Child's Health History (continued)

V. FAMILY HISTORY (see list of conditions on reverse)

SIBLINGS (note if half sibling)					PARENTS	
AGE	SEX	MAJOR HEALTH PROBLEMS (or cause of death)	RELATION	AGE	MAJOR HEALTH PROBLEMS (or cause of death)	
			MOTHER			
			HER FATHER			
			HER MOTHER			
			FATHER			
			HIS MOTHER			
			HIS FATHER			

VI. SOURCE OF INFORMATION:
☐ MOTHER ☐ FATHER ☐ OTHER (specify below)

VII. ☐ ADDITIONAL CONFIDENTIAL INFORMATION AVAILABLE FROM CHILD'S WORKER

VIII. COMMENTS (including other significant history in aunts, uncles, and blood cousins)

Figure 5. Maryland Health Passport: Instructions

MARK "X" IN THE APPROPRIATE BOX FOR ALL SECTIONS.

WHEN TO COMPLETE: At intake, when a child is removed and placed out of the home of the parent or legal guardian.

WHO COMPLETES: The worker who initiates the removal from the home of the parent or legal guardian into placement. Additional information should be added by subsequent workers as information becomes known.

Medical records should be requested if information is not provided by parent, legal guardian, or caretaker.

Prenatal/Birth: Complete items 1–5 for child under 5 years old. Complete items 6–9 for all children.

Immunizations: Complete for immunizations prior to entry into care and update as appropriate.

Family History: Indicate any major health problems, such as

Birth defects	Mental retardation
Congenital heart defects	Learning disabilities
Cleft lip/palate	Mental illness (specify)
Spina bifida	Alcoholism
Kidney disease	Childhood orthopedic problems (specify)
Curved spine	Childhood muscle problems
Heart disease	Diabetes
Cancer (specify)	Childhood deafness
Down syndrome	Childhood blindness
Cystic fibrosis	
HIV*	

* *If parent has tested HIV+, note on case record copy only and check the box in Section VII marked "Additional confidential information is available..."*

VI. This sections MUST be completed. "Other" may include child's relatives, caretaker, case or medical records. Check all that apply.

The Maryland Health Passport is a good example of a "minimalist" approach to genetic family histories. The form is simple. It guides the child welfare worker by listing more common genetic conditions. Workers who have not had genetics training can use the form. True, the information will be incomplete; a genetics professional would know how to obtain a fuller history. It is not feasible, however, to arrange for a genetics professional to see every child under child welfare supervision. The Maryland Health Passport makes it possible to screen for clients who might benefit from one or another genetic service.

Constructing a Pedigree

Genetic professionals usually record GFHs on a diagram they refer to as a *pedigree*. You may already know how to construct a genogram. A pedigree is similar to a genogram, except that it emphasizes health information.

We suggest that you learn how to construct a pedigree diagram. Figure 6 presents commonly used symbols. Figure 7 provides directions for recording the pedigree. You might suggest that your agency arrange for in-service training in genetics; you might also suggest genetics training to your local social work continuing education sponsor, such as your state chapter of the National Association of Social Workers or a school of social work.

Pedigrees have advantages over other ways of recording GFHs. They are concise, and they present the data visually in an easily understood format. Most physicians are familiar with pedigree diagrams and can assist in their interpretation. Pedigrees can be easily expanded if additional family history information becomes available. They eliminate the need to decipher and organize GFH information buried in lists or in narrative sections of a case record. Construction of a pedigree should begin with drawing the basic family structure. A standard form may be used for recording the pedigree (Figure 8).

Recording the Information 59

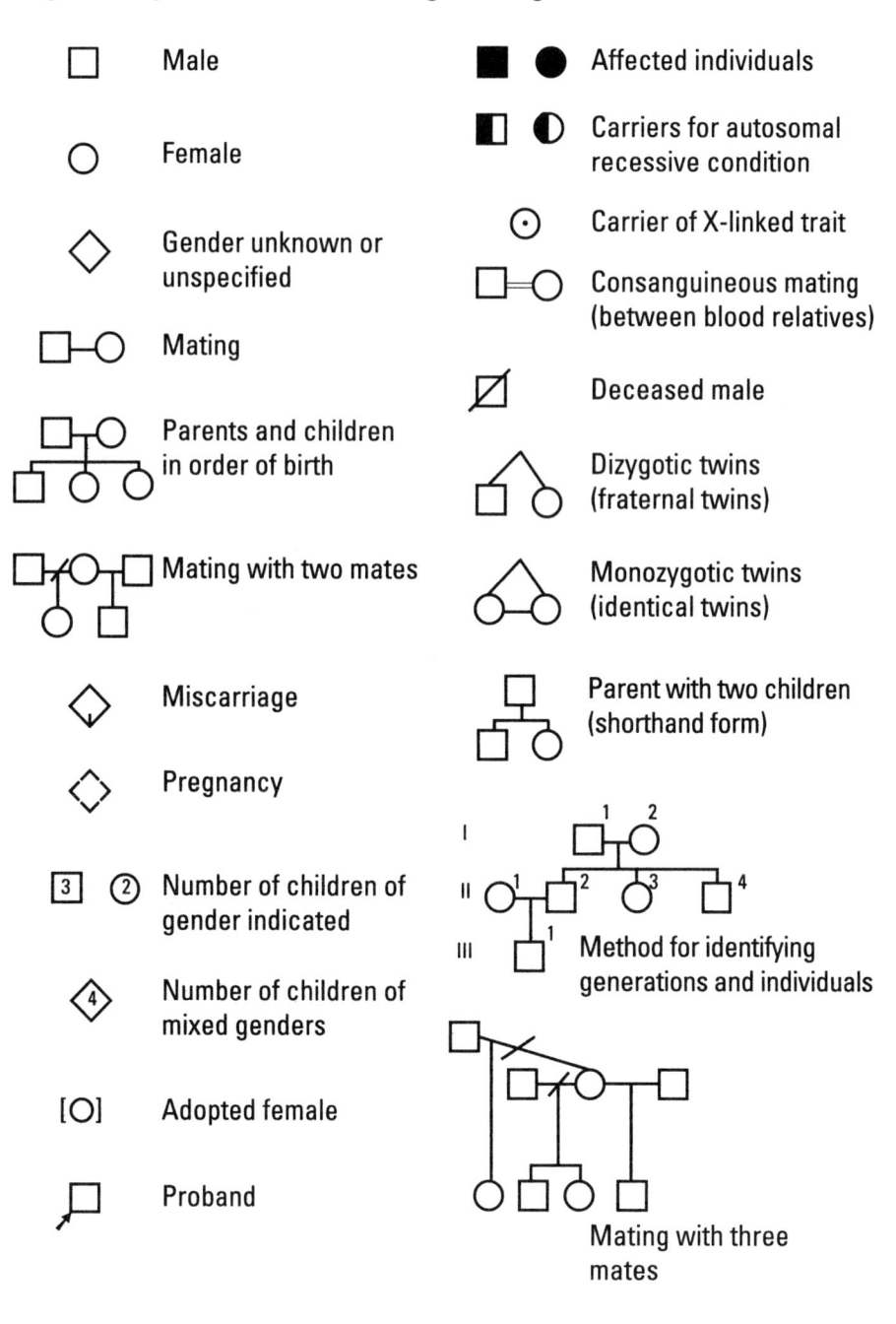

Figure 6. Symbols Used in a Pedigree Diagram

□	Male	■ ●	Affected individuals
○	Female	◨ ◐	Carriers for autosomal recessive condition
◇	Gender unknown or unspecified	⊙	Carrier of X-linked trait
□─○	Mating	□═○	Consanguineous mating (between blood relatives)
	Parents and children in order of birth	⊠	Deceased male
	Mating with two mates		Dizygotic twins (fraternal twins)
◇	Miscarriage		Monozygotic twins (identical twins)
◇	Pregnancy		Parent with two children (shorthand form)
③ ②	Number of children of gender indicated		Method for identifying generations and individuals
④	Number of children of mixed genders		
[○]	Adopted female		
⌐□	Proband		Mating with three mates

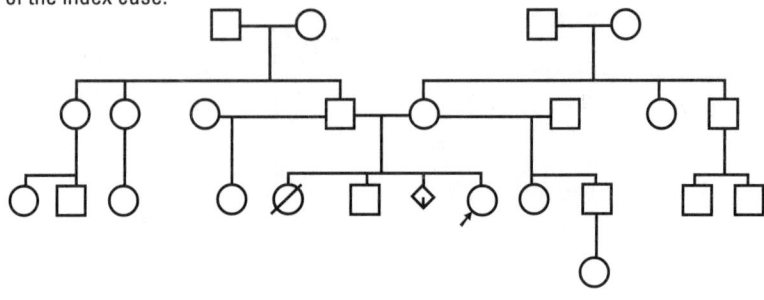

Figure 7. Directions for Drawing a Pedigree Diagram

1. The index case (the child being considered for adoption) is placed in the middle of the bottom of the page and designated with an arrow. Males are represented by squares and females by circles.

2. Record all the index case's full brothers and sisters in birth order (oldest on the right, youngest on the left), including deceased siblings and additional pregnancies that ended in miscarriages. Use a branched bar to connect siblings.

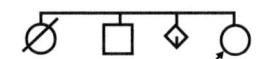

3. Draw the parents, male partner on the left and female partner on the right and connect them with a mating line.

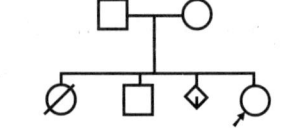

4. Add half siblings and their parents.
5. Indicate birth dates, birth years, or ages for all individuals.
6. If there are any, draw in nieces or nephews of the index case.

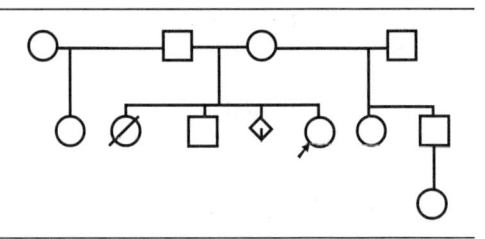

7. Expand the pedigree to aunts, uncles, cousins, and grandparents of the index case.

Recording the Information

Figure 8. Form for Recording a Pedigree Diagram

□	= male
○	= female
◇	= gender unknown
○—□	= mating
○—□ (with sibling line)	= fraternal twins
⊠	= dead
◇ with p	= pregnancy
● ◆ ■	= abortions or stillbirths
○=□	= consanguineous mating
(triangle with twins)	= identical twins
■	= affected
◨	= heterozygote autosomal recessive
⊙	= carrier X-linked recessive

Medical Genetic Family Pedigree

Propositus _____

Date _____

Recorder _____

Informant _____

MR/LD	Seizures	Kidney
MCA	Skeletal	Muscle (neuro)
NTD	Blindness	Blood (anemia)
Cancer	Deafness	Heart (congenital, early M.I.)
Thyroid	Psychiatric	Stillbirth, infant death

Information to Include on the Pedigree Diagram

- Document the country of origin (ethnicity) of each grandparent or his or her family.
- Note whether the parents of the index case (client) are blood relatives and, if so, indicate relationship.
- Indicate cause and age of death of all deceased individuals.
- Indicate health problems or pertinent medical information below the pedigree symbol of any relative.
- Ask about unusual health problems, birth defects, genetic disorders, or mental retardation in more distant relatives, and include those individuals who are affected. Gender is important.
- Individuals affected with a particular trait should be colored in and a key added to the pedigree indicating the significance of the symbol. Other symbols, such as crosshatching pedigree symbols may be used to designate other disorders or traits, but their significance must be documented in the key. A complete pedigree is shown in Figure 9. This form for recording a pedigree diagram is an 8 1/2" x 11" sheet, with space left to fill in the entire pedigree.
- Family history issues can be sensitive in some cases. Questions should be asked in a sensitive, nonjudgmental manner, using language that the client can understand.

It may be easier to get important genetic information by using a form with specific questions about genetic disorders, such as the long genetic history form in Appendix B. Information from the form can be transferred to the pedigree after the basic family structure is drawn. For family members with an extensive medical history, narrative information may be attached on a separate sheet.

Figure 9. Example of a Completed Pedigree Diagram

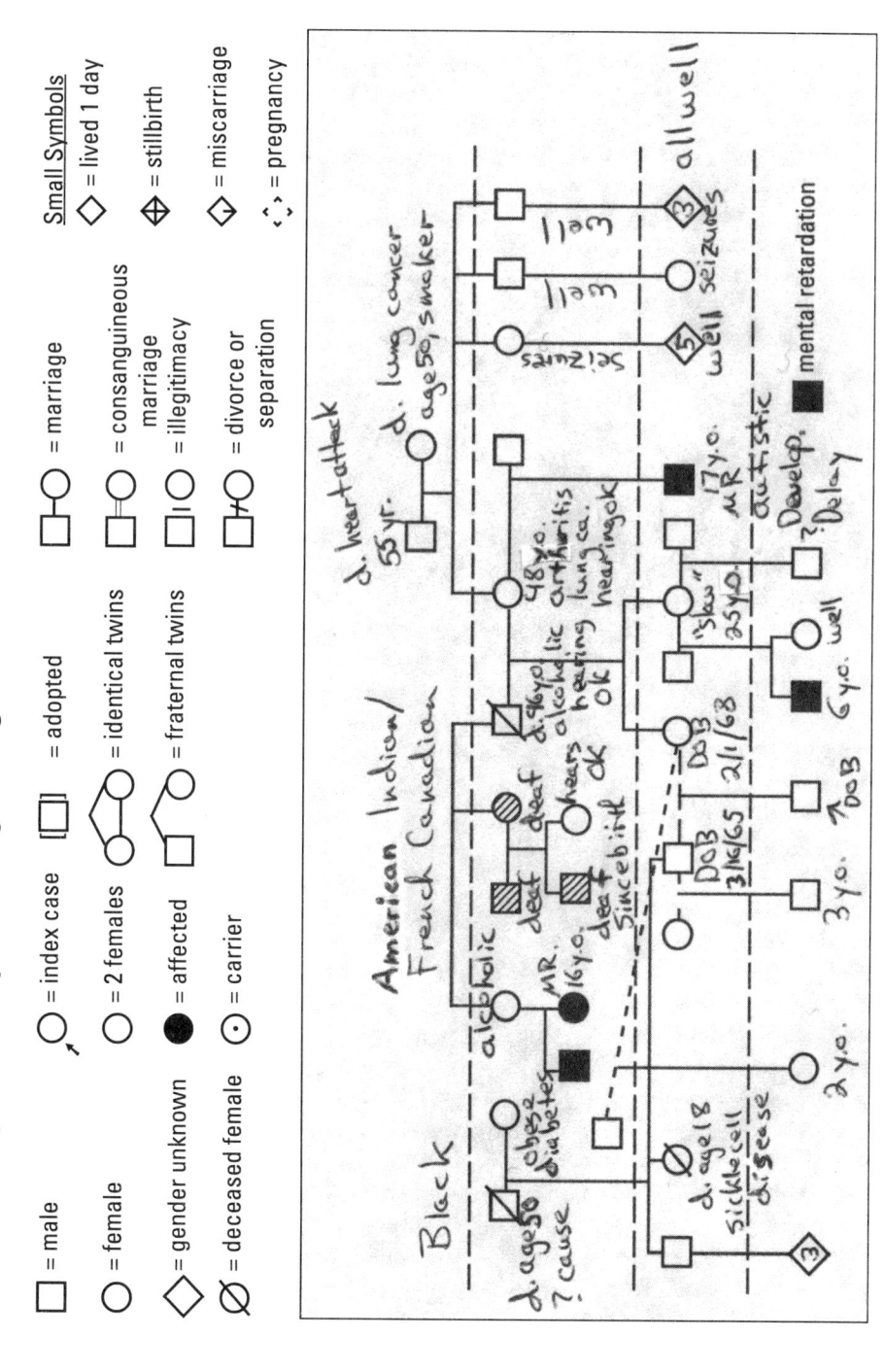

□ = male	○↙ = index case	□—□ = adopted
○ = female	○ = 2 females	◇◇ = identical twins
◇ = gender unknown	● = affected	◇◇ = fraternal twins
⊘ = deceased female	⊙ = carrier	

□—○ = marriage	**Small Symbols**
□═○ = consanguineous marriage	◇ = lived 1 day
□—○ = illegitimacy	⊕ = stillbirth
□⊬○ = divorce or separation	◇ = miscarriage
	⟨⟩ = pregnancy

Chapter 8

Transmitting the Information

Complexity of Genetic Information

Transmitting genetic information has two components: presentation and comprehension. Genetic information is complex and difficult to interpret. People often do not correctly understand it. For example, with certain single gene disorders, chances are one-in-four with each conception that the child will inherit the faulty gene from both parents and have the disorder. Some people think that this means that if their first child has the disorder, the next three children will be healthy. That belief is mistaken. Chances are one-in-four with *each* conception, not one-in-four of all children in a family. Because each conception is an independent throw of the dice, so to speak, all children of two carrier parents could be affected. Similarly, carrier parents might have no affected children.

> Mr. and Mrs. S. had five children. Four were sons who had cystic fibrosis.

> Mr. and Mrs. T. had seven children. The first six were healthy. The seventh had cystic fibrosis. If Mr. and Mrs. T. had stopped at six children, they would never have known that they both carried the CF gene. Their brothers and sisters would not have known that they might also carry the CF gene.

Genetic information must be presented simply and clearly, in terms that even poorly educated people can understand. Presenting genetic information so that it can be understood is a skill. The information should be repeated and presented in different ways—for example, verbally, in a brochure, and in a written letter. Steps must be taken, such as asking for feedback, to make sure that the information is understood. The information should be accurate and up-to-date.

Comprehend is a critical word. There are several barriers to comprehending genetic information. One is the complexity of the information. Another is poor presentation—use of specialized terminology, presentation of too much information, or failure to ask for feedback. Another is that the listener may be unable to absorb the information due to anxiety or discomfort about asking questions. Some potential adoptive parents do not "hear" the information because they want a child so much that they block out negative information. An important part of the social worker's job is to be sure that the information is understood and that its potential ramifications have been explored. This takes time and the willingness to stay with the issues. The information may have to be presented several times.

Adoption

Genetic information should be presented in graduated doses over time. Potential adoptive parents should be educated about inheritance and psychosocial aspects of genetic disorders early in the adoption process, before being presented with a specific child. A good time to provide this information is during the group orientation, if your agency uses groups. An array of written resources is available, ranging from paperbacks for the general public to brochures published by organizations concerned with genetic disorders. Unfortunately, to the best of our knowledge, no good audiovisual resource suited for parent training is currently available. Parents of children with genetic disorders are an invaluable resource who can discuss what it is like to care for a child with special health care needs.

Transmitting genetic information depends on an effective partnership between child welfare agencies and genetic professionals. Genetic professionals can conduct parent orientation groups on genetics. You can turn to them with questions that you might have about specific situations. They can provide genetic counseling. Importantly, they can conduct agency in-service training in genetics. In general, genetic professionals consider educating the public and other professionals to be an important responsibility, and they are ready to cooperate with child welfare workers and agencies. Some genetic professionals will be associated with universities that have the capacity to provide training or consultation to rural or isolated areas via interactive television.

Genetic Diagnoses and Biological Family Members

Should biological relatives be told about a genetic diagnosis in a child who has been adopted away? What about the converse? If a genetic disorder is discovered in the biological family of an adopted child, should the adoptive parents or the adult adoptee be informed? Both are complex issues that pertain to law, ethics, and the confidentiality of child welfare, adoption, and medical records [Lamport 1988; Omenn et al. 1980].

With genetic information, issues of privacy are offset by others' rights and needs to know. In some instances, a genetic diagnosis is significant to the health and well-being of biological relatives and their offspring. Knowledge of genetic risk may be, in some instances, lifesaving; lack of knowledge may be life-threatening. Do professionals have a duty to inform, just as there is a duty to inform a potential victim if a client is threatening to commit murder?

Many geneticists have been concerned about whether to inform biological relatives, adoptive parents, and adult adoptees about a diagnosis when written consent to release information cannot be obtained or, conversely, biological relatives have not indicated an interest in obtaining health or genetic information. Fortunately, most health care facilities have ethics committees and lawyers with whom geneticists can consult in such situations. If you happen to encounter a situation in which others' rights and needs to know conflict with confidentiality, the genetic professionals involved are likely to seek ethical and legal consultation. You should not neglect your independent responsibilities, however. In such situations, you and your agency may want to obtain legal and ethical consultation. Unfortunately, there are as yet no agreed-upon guidelines. Even when guidelines are established, they are open to interpretation. We encourage you to seek consultation when you are involved in situations in which there are conflicts between confidentiality and others' needs or rights to know.

II

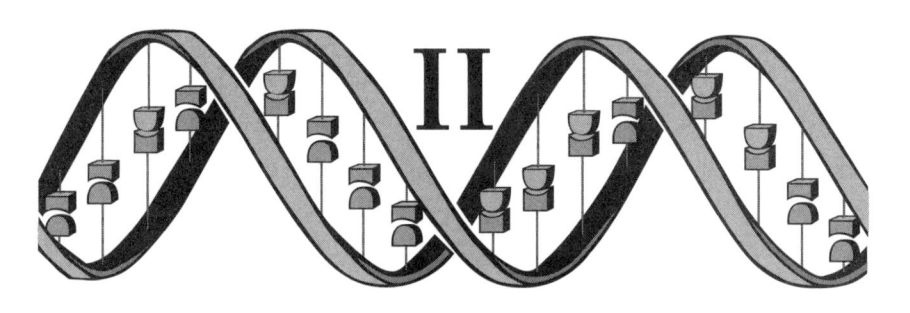

Genetics and Child Welfare

Chapter 9
Self-Awareness and Self-Directed Learning

Depending on how serious they are, genetic disorders are usually stressful for affected individuals and their families. Although many, perhaps most, families cope successfully, living with genetic disorders can interfere with children's' psychosocial development and strain families' coping capacities. Remember, children with special health care needs—many of which are genetic—are more likely than other children to come under child welfare supervision [Garbarino et al. 1986; U.S. General Accounting Office 1995; Pinkney 1994].

Psychosocial functioning and physical health mutually affect each other [Rolland 1994]. Psychosocial stress appears to affect immune functioning, increase susceptibility to disease, and worsen existing health problems. In addition, a child may not do well medically if family stress interferes with a caregivers' ability to provide adequate care. Stress may generate new problems for the affected individual as well as for other family members.

> Amiel, 17, had liver disease. Since being diagnosed when he was 15 months old, Amiel and his parents lived with the prospect of his imminent death. When he was 10, Amiel was one of the first persons to receive a liver transplant. The constant fear of possible transplant rejection and death presented major problems for the entire family. Amiel's steroid treatment to prevent rejection prevented puberty. His condition worsened over time, and his body became yellow and swollen. Teachers and classmates thought he looked strange; he was unable to make friends.

Amiel was unable to voice his feelings of sadness, loneliness, and anxiety about dying. He engaged in explosive outbursts and obsessive handwashing and showering. In addition, his 15-year-old sister, Dorinda, whose needs had been neglected because of her parents' absorption in Amiel, did poorly in school, began to use drugs, and was sexually promiscuous. The parents quarreled over how to discipline Dorinda, creating tension in their relationship.

Differentness Self-Awareness

Some child welfare workers do not work as effectively with children who have genetic disorders and their families as do others, often because they are awkward and uncomfortable with "differentness." They may unconsciously transmit their discomfort to the affected individuals and their families. A trusting relationship becomes difficult if not impossible to establish. For this reason, you should be

- aware of your attitudes toward people with chronic illnesses and disabilities, especially when the cause is genetic;
- aware of how your attitudes may affect your behavior; and
- able to moderate your feelings and behavior so you can make individuals with genetic disorders and their families feel accepted and valued.

This chapter is intended to help you become more aware of your feelings towards people with genetic disorders. Once you identify potentially problematic perceptions and attitudes, the next step is to try to change them.

Getting accurate information is important toward attitude change. So is becoming acquainted with genetically affected individuals and families. Although you can learn a lot from families in your caseload, we encourage you to seek out other individuals and families who have coped successfully. They will be able to give you insights and information you can use to better help your clients.

Identifying Your Attitudes

Differentness

Most of us have feelings about people who are different from us. Sometimes we feel just a little bit uncomfortable and awkward, not sure of what to say or do. We may find that we cannot look at a child who is physically deformed—or, conversely, we may be unable to stop staring. Some people are afraid of adolescents who are mentally retarded or mentally ill. People who use wheelchairs often complain that others treat them as though they were invisible. Many people avoid dying friends because they don't know what to say or do. Some social workers avoid contact with children who are chronically ill or disabled because they find seeing them unbearably painful. Perhaps worst of all, some of us pity people with serious illnesses or disabilities. We do not see the person; we ignore his or her strengths, capacities, and potential, and we hold out few, if any, expectations.

Because feelings affect behavior, it is important to be aware of your attitudes. You may find that your feelings are balanced and appropriate. On the other hand, you may be embarrassed or ashamed of some of the feelings you identify. Remember that honesty is better than pretending that you only have "good" or "the right" attitudes. Honest self-awareness will enable you to be a better practitioner.

Your Genetic Disorders Biography

One way to identify the sources of your attitudes is to look at your past experiences. Exercise 5, on page 83, will help you create your own genetic disorders biography. We suggest that you do this exercise even if you yourself do not have a genetic disorder.

Attitudes Continuum

One way to think about attitudes towards people with genetic disorders is that your feelings are on a continuum from, at the negative end, actively destructive to, at the positive end, deep respect (see Figure 10, page 74). After reading the description of the points on the continuum, locate yourself on it.

Figure 10. Attitude Continuum

Destructive   Incapable   Unaware   Ready to learn   Respectful

Actively Destructive

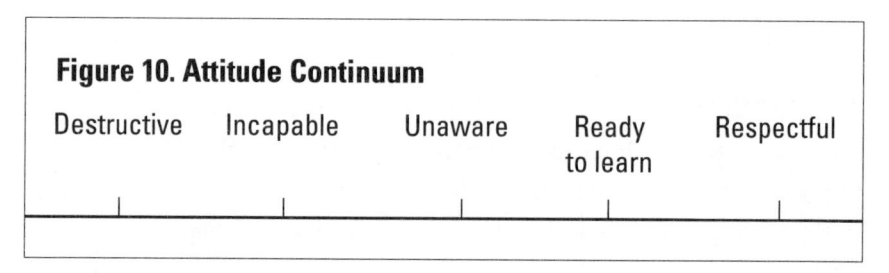

Actively destructive persons or social agencies see people with genetic disorders as inferior to other people, seek to block specialized programs to meet their needs, and are *eugenicists* or *eugenistic*—they believe steps should be taken to reduce the number of people with genetic disorders, such as sterilizing people with certain genetic characteristics or aborting fetuses with certain genetic disorders. In the past, destructive U.S. policies and practices included warehousing in institutions and involuntary sterilization [Kevles 1985] of people who were mentally retarded or mentally ill. Although things have improved, too many vulnerable children, adolescents, and adults are in destructive settings in which they are physically restrained and abused.

Some observers are concerned that subtle pressures are exerted on people at reproductive risk to become sterilized or to terminate pregnancies if the fetus has a genetic disorder [Garver & Garver 1994]. In addition, employment and insurance discrimination against people with genetic disorders, known carriers of genes for genetic disorders, and families with histories of genetic disorders has been documented [Billings 1992; Natowicz et al. 1992]. We consider advocates of such policies as being at the destructive end of the attitude continuum.

Incapable

The *incapable* worker or agency also believes that people with genetic disorders are undesirable. They send subtle messages that they are not valued and that little is expected of them. Staff do not try to understand such clients or to provide services that would help them realize their potential. The agency does not provide its staff with human genetics training.

Some special education settings are incapable. They are little more than means of segregating from other children those who are different or who are seen as "problems." Children with different educational needs are jumbled together in overly large classes. Poorly maintained and unattractive physical facilities convey the message that these students don't count. Overwhelmed teachers are unable to provide quality, individualized instruction. Social agencies may also be incapable.

> Mrs. O. sought counseling from a family and children's agency. She was concerned about the influence of her neighborhood on her 13-year-old son, Aaron, who was mildly mentally retarded. Ms. O. and Aaron lived in an urban neighborhood with rampant crime and violence. Aaron was skipping school and hanging out with older youths who had dropped out of school and were, in Mrs. O.'s words, "up to no good." Ms. O. worried that Aaron might get into trouble because he was easily led by others. The worker concluded that Ms. O. was overprotective and that Aaron was appropriately trying to separate from his mother. She recommended family therapy targeted at the family enmeshment. Mrs. O. did not return for a second appointment.

Unaware

Agencies and workers who are *unaware* are well-intentioned but assume that all people have the same needs and can be helped with the same modalities. They attempt to incorporate clients with genetic disorders into existing services. They do not recognize that services may need to be adapted to meet the needs of this group of clients. When clients' characteristics and the services provided do not fit well together, the unaware agency or worker focuses on the clients' characteristics. "Bobby is home bound and so cannot participate in our socialization group." "Mr. T. has a severe speech impediment and is not a candidate for psychotherapy." Unaware agencies and workers do not question their practices, nor see that services may need to be adapted or expanded. They also lack avenues for obtaining feedback about the shortcomings of their services.

According to law, policy, and regulations, a state department of child, youth, and family services required that a genetic family history be obtained for each child in out-of-home care, if obtainable. The agency did not train its workers in genetics, however, nor in how to obtain such a history. The agency also did not offer training in disorders that had high incidences in its clientele, such as ADHD, asthma, diabetes, fetal alcohol syndrome, learning disabilities, and mental retardation.

Ready to Learn

Agencies and workers who are *ready to learn* recognize their weaknesses, desire to improve, and take steps to do so. An agency, for example, might offer in-service training in genetic disorders or recruit an expert in genetic disorders for its board. Individual workers may read about genetic disorders or go to relevant workshops and conferences. To their credit, these agencies and workers have identified a problem and taken steps to remedy it. Efforts at change may not be maintained, however, if they do not succeed initially, if obstacles occur, or if a key agent of change leaves the agency.

After their 8-year-old daughter was diagnosed with childhood schizophrenia, Mr. and Mrs. K. sued their county child welfare agency for wrongful adoption on the basis that it withheld information that their daughter's biological mother was diagnosed with paranoid schizophrenia. In response, the director instituted training in state law and regulations pertaining to information disclosure in adoptions, genetics, taking genetic family histories, and agency procedures for information disclosure. After the director left the agency, however, her successor discontinued the training when funds were cut.

Respect

Genuine respect is the highest level on the continuum. At this stage, agencies respect people with genetic disorders and their families. They regard parents as partners and the true experts on their children's needs. Respectful agencies have mechanisms for client input into services. Affected persons and members of their families may be hired as staff or recruited as volunteers and trained to provide support services. Respectful agencies and workers engage in ongoing self-assessment, expand their knowledge of genetic disorders and their psychosocial impacts, adapt their services to fit clients' needs, and advocate for improved programs and policies.

> A city child welfare department realized that many of the children who were referred for neglect and abuse had special health care needs. It selected the community with the highest rate of referrals to Child Protective Services to institute a foster grandmother program. Older women who had already raised their children were trained as pediatric home health aides and case managers. They were included on the family preservation team that worked with families who had special needs children. Foster grandmothers assisted with daily care, offered emotional support, helped caregivers access needed services, and provided respite care. The agency sponsored regular training and case conferences to increase staff's knowledge of chronic illnesses and disabilities in children and adolescents. Program evaluation documented that incidences of neglect and abuse of children with special health care needs decreased significantly.

You and the Continuum

Where are you located on the continuum? If you are not yet ready for learning, you may lack awareness, be misinformed, be influenced by stereotypes, or have gaps in your knowledge. If so, you can do much to increase your awareness and knowledge. Perhaps painful life experiences make you withdraw from people with genetic disorders or one specific disorder. In that case, talking with someone you trust might be helpful. Psychotherapy might be beneficial if your experiences with people with genetic disorders were traumatic or associated with complex family issues. Do you have bottled-up genetic concerns?

Sometimes it is not possible to change our feelings much. Sometimes it is better to say "I can't deal with this" and ask that a situation be assigned to someone else if it touches on issues that are deeply painful for you and may interfere with your ability to help.

> Ms. L., a foster care worker, was assigned the case of Jamal W., a 15-year-old with sickle cell disease who was doing poorly. Ms. L.'s brother had died three years earlier of sickle cell disease, when he, too, was 15. Just learning about Jamal aroused her grief over her brother's death. She recognized that her grief would interfere with her ability to help Jamal cope with his situation, so she asked that Jamal be assigned to another worker. Her supervisor agreed.

If you are at the ready-to-learn stage, then you have already recognized a need to learn. No matter where you are on the continuum, remember that change is a step-by-step process. (See Figure 11.) If you are open to change and growth, you will always be "in process," even when you reach the competent stage.

Self-Directed Learning

Reading

There are two main groupings of books and articles: those dealing with chronic illnesses and disabilities in children and adolescents in general, and those dealing with specific disorders. Some resources are intended for health professionals in general; others are written specifically for social workers. Many are directed at parents and other family members, including youngsters, and can be obtained by contacting information clearinghouses. (See Appendix D.) So-called women's magazines often contain articles about specific conditions or narratives of how individuals have coped with serious health problems in themselves or their children.

Appendix E lists some books and articles for a social work audience. If your local library does not have them, its interlibrary loan department should be able to obtain them for you for a small fee.

Figure 11. Learning Steps

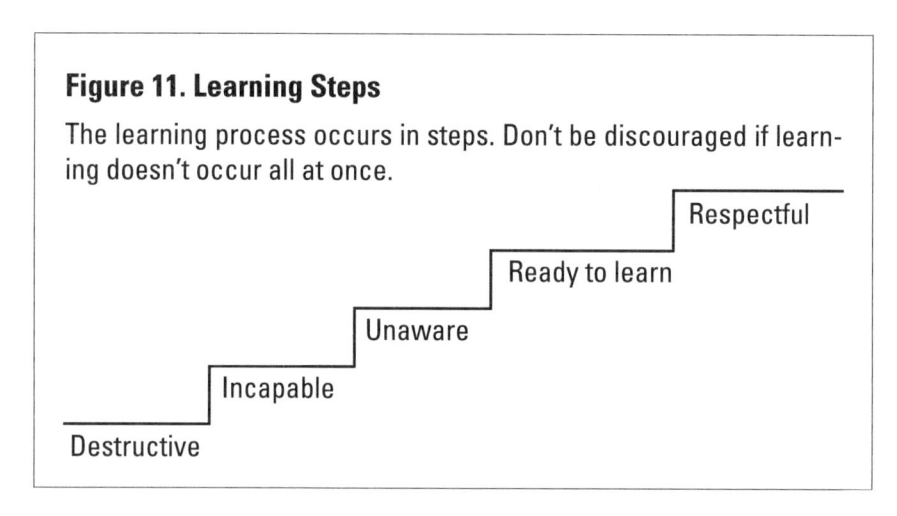

The learning process occurs in steps. Don't be discouraged if learning doesn't occur all at once.

```
                                    Respectful
                       Ready to learn
              Unaware
    Incapable
Destructive
```

Organizations concerned with children's health or with specific health problems frequently have pamphlets, videotapes, and speakers available, often at no cost. (See Appendix A.) Bookstores' health sections often carry books concerned with more common disorders.

Do not limit yourself to books and articles written for professionals. You can learn much from materials directed at parents. Reading books intended for children and adolescents will give you insight into their experiences and may also suggest helpful ways of framing your comments to child and adolescent clients who have genetic disorders.

Movies and Videotapes

Some commercial movies and television shows have told stories of individuals and families affected by genetic disorders. In *Rainman*, for example, Dustin Hoffman plays a man who is autistic. Other movies dealing with genetic disorders include *Lorenzo's Oil, My Left Foot, Forrest Gump,* and *The Elephant Man.* Medical television shows, such as *Chicago Hope;* soap operas; and dramatic series sometimes feature genetic conditions or issues. Watch commercial movies and television shows critically, however. Often, they sentimentalize, overdramatize, or otherwise distort reality. Even so, movies and television shows can provide useful information and help to humanize people affected by genetic disorders.

Organizations concerned with genetic disorders in general, such as the March of Dimes, or with specific disorders, can be invaluable sources of videotapes intended for families or professionals. Some may be in your public library's video collection. If you are near a major university, your agency may be able to borrow tapes from the media libraries of the schools of social work, nursing, medicine, and others. Some hospitals have media collections, especially if they are sites for training health professionals. If you cannot locate relevant tapes locally, they are usually available for mail purchase or rental from sponsoring organizations at modest costs.

Learning by Doing

As you know, learning by *doing* is often more effective than other ways of learning. With a little creativity, you can develop some excellent learning activities for yourself, including some that can be performed as part of your job. Here are some possibilities:

- Attend an educational planning meeting for a child with special educational needs.
- Attend a meeting of a genetics support group.
- Try to get SSI for a child with a genetic disorder.
- Spend a day shadowing a caregiver of a child with a genetic condition to get a feel for the caregiver's daily routine.
- Accompany a child to a genetics evaluation.
- Go with a child or adolescent who has a genetic condition to an appointment at a clinic that provides his or her specialty care.
- Interview an older adolescent or adult with a genetic condition; ask what it was like to grow up with the condition and how he or she thinks you can best help a child with a similar condition.
- Spend a day in a wheelchair (if you can borrow one).
- For one week, follow a diet in which you or your family members eat no wheat and wheat products.
- Invite a community group, such as the Association for Retarded Citizens, to present a panel of individuals and families affected by genetic disorders who are willing to share how they can best be helped.
- Brainstorm other ideas of your own!

Exercise 4. Differentness Self-Awareness

What are your feelings about differentness? Answer the questions below. Give your first, spontaneous responses, without censoring them.

1. When I see a child with cerebral palsy, I usually _____
   _____

2. An adolescent with schizophrenia is _____
   _____

3. If I had a child who was mentally retarded, I would _____
   _____

4. The last time I saw a child in a wheelchair, I _____
   _____

5. Children with chronic illnesses usually _____
   _____

6. If I were standing next to a blind adolescent at a red light on a busy street, and he did not have a guide dog, I would _____
   _____

7. If someone uses a negative word for people who are different, such as "retard" or "crip," I usually _____
   _____

8. If I (or my significant other) were pregnant with a baby with Down syndrome, I would _____
   _____

9. If a 9-year-old who had a fatal illness told me that he was afraid of dying, I would _____

_____

10. The first time I became aware of people with disabilities was

_____

My reaction was _____

_____

Look at your answers to Exercise 4. Do they suggest situations that are uncomfortable for you? Groups of people about whom you have strong negative feelings? Patterns of behavior you would like to change? A helpful way to end this exercise is to select the three situations or responses that are most difficult for you. Try to figure out why you have those feelings by talking with someone you trust. You can also write a memo to yourself to identify the basis of your attitudes. Perhaps you are a shy person who is uncomfortable with new people and situations. Perhaps your family treated serious health problems as taboo topics. Perhaps personal experiences have shaped your attitudes. Don't overlook how other people, the media, and U.S. culture may affect you. For example, stereotypes and negative feelings about people who are mentally retarded are quite common.

Exercise 5. Your Genetic Disorders Biography

1. Using the form below, enter a plus sign (+) for each setting in which you had a positive experience with a person with an inherited disease, a developmental disability, or another disability (such as blindness). Use a minus sign (-) for settings in which you had a negative experience. For settings in which you had a mixed experience, enter a plus and a minus sign (+/-).

	Inherited Disease	Developmental Disability	Other Disability
Family/Preschool			
K–6			
Middle School			
High School			
College/Grad School			
Military			
Work			
Personal Relationships			
Neighborhood			
Travel			
Born/Live Outside U.S.			

What does the pattern of your responses suggest about the extent of your interactions with people with genetic diseases, developmental disabilities, or other disabilities?

2. Check any of the following statements that are true:

   ☐ There is no known genetic disorder or genetic risk in myself or my family.

   ☐ I carry, or may carry, a gene for a genetic disorder.

   ☐ There is a known or suspected genetic disorder in my family.

   ☐ I have a genetic disorder.

   ☐ My child(ren) has/have a genetic disorder.

3. Complete the following statement:

   My genetic status and genetic biography suggest that when I am working with children with genetic disorders, their siblings, and their caregivers, I may _____.

   After you have completed this exercise, ask yourself what you have learned about your experiences with people with genetic conditions. Is your experience limited, or have you known many people with genetic disorders? Has your experience been largely with acquaintances, or has it involved close friends and family members? On the whole, have your experiences been positive or negative? How might your experiences have contributed to your attitudes toward people with genetic disorders in general or people with specific disorders?

Exercise 6. Current Relationships

Another way of looking at things that contribute to your perceptions and attitudes about people with genetic disorders is to look at their place in your current life.

Directions

1. Exercise 6 contains two overlapping circles. In the right circle, enter the names of *people you are close* to who *do not have* a genetic disorder.
2. In the overlapping section, list *people you are close to* who *have* a genetic disorder. For each, indicate if the condition is an illness or disability. How serious is the condition? Is it stigmatized?
3. In the left circle, enter the names of *people you know but are not close to* who *have* a genetic disorder. For each, indicate if the condition is an illness or disability. How serious is the condition? Is it stigmatized?

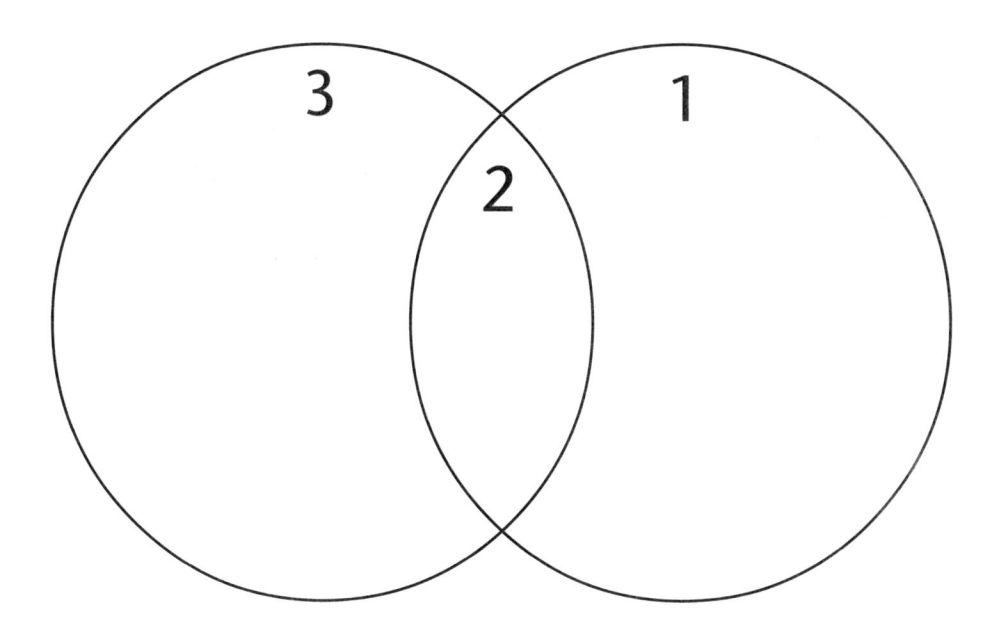

Some Questions

1. What does the pattern of your current relationships tell you about your connectedness to people with genetic disorders?

2. With what types of genetic disorders are you familiar, if any?

3. How might the closeness or distance of your relationships with people with genetic disorders affect your general perceptions of people with genetic disorders, your feelings about them, and your comfort with differentness?

4. Have your contacts been mainly with clients? If so, how might that affect your perceptions and attitudes?

5. What does the pattern tell you about your current connectedness to people with genetic disorders? How might that affect your perceptions of people with genetic disorders, your feelings about them, and your understanding of their situations?

Chapter 10
Genetic Disorders and Child Development

Children with genetic disorders face the same developmental tasks as healthy children. Mastery of these tasks, however, and successful coping with the usual stresses of childhood are more difficult for them. The ongoing presence of a serious genetic disorder can significantly affect aspects of the child's physical and mental functioning and his or her interactions with other people and the environment. The specific impact is shaped by many factors, including a caregiver's ability to provide a safe, nurturing environment; the child's age; and the child's stage of development.

Erikson's [1963] stages of psychosocial development provide one framework for thinking about child and adolescent development. Erikson states that children pass through fixed developmental stages. Each stage has a "crisis," or developmental task, that must be resolved or mastered.

- **Infancy** (approximately birth to age 2 years). Developmental task: Trust versus mistrust
- **Early childhood** (approximately age 2 to 4 years). Developmental task: Autonomy versus shame
- **Play age** (approximately age 4 to 6 years). Developmental task: Initiative versus guilt
- **School age** (approximately age 6 to 12 years). Developmental task: Industry versus inferiority
- **Adolescence** (approximately age 12 to 18 years). Developmental task: Identity versus identity confusion

How the child resolves the crisis or completes the developmental task sets the stage for future psychosocial development. For example, the major developmental task of infancy is developing basic trust. Children who succeed in this task have a good foundation for future psychosocial development. Those who develop basic mistrust are off to a poor start in life.

In this chapter, we use Erikson's model to frame our discussion of the psychosocial impact of genetic disorders on child development. The goal of intervention should be *normalization*, that is, enabling the child to develop as normally as possible.

Infancy: Basic Trust Versus Basic Mistrust

Most caregivers handle babies with genetic disorders pretty well. In general, the babies do okay and even thrive, within their capacities. In the best of circumstances, however, caring for infants is demanding. It is even more demanding to care for babies with serious genetic disorders.

According to Erikson [1963], basic trust evolves in a safe world that offers consistency, continuity, and sameness of experience. The baby must become attached to a stable, dependable, responsive caretaker.

Babies born with genetic conditions may be denied needed consistency and safety. They may be hospitalized for long periods of time. Even though most hospitals today welcome parents and encourage them to participate in their child's care, hospitalization still often involves separation from the parents. Parents may be unable to come to the hospital because of distance or other responsibilities; they may need to leave at times, if only to go home to sleep at night.

In the hospital, the baby is likely to experience painful medical procedures, intense stimulation such as the continuous noise of monitors or ventilators, and multiple caregivers. Indeed, parents may feel that the baby belongs to the medical staff. When they are at the hospital, the parents may be anxious, tense, and unable to interact comfortably with their baby. If the baby looks unusual, disappointed parents may avoid visiting.

When there is a chance that their baby might die, some parents protect themselves emotionally against loss by not bonding with the baby. Some parents may feel intimidated by the need to learn how to perform complicated procedures to be allowed to take their child home. They may be terrified of taking the child home. Such experiences may make it difficult for babies to bond with their parents.

Even if an infant is not hospitalized and is cared for at home, symptoms of the genetic disorder and home care regimens may affect her psychosocial development. The baby may experience pain, discomfort, or continuous hunger. She may be subjected to painful procedures, uncomfortable equipment, or restriction of movement.

Infant-caretaker attachment may be hindered. Sickly infants may not interact with other people due to lethargy or fatigue. A caregiver may also feel rejected by the baby—for example, if the infant does not respond to efforts to soothe or comfort. Some children with disabilities have persistent and irritating cries. A caregiver might interact less with an unresponsive, "rejecting," or irritating baby because the interaction is unrewarding.

Unresponsive or difficult babies may be especially stressful for caregivers who are cognitively or emotionally limited or who are socially isolated. Thus, a nonhospitalized infant may, like the hospitalized one, be in a situation that hinders the development of basic trust. In addition, the child's condition may limit ability to explore the world and practice new abilities. Cognitive and motor development may be delayed or impaired.

A diagnosis in infancy may carry a lot of unknowns about the severity of the child's condition and his care requirements and outcome. Entering parenthood with a platter full of unknowns is not easy. Babies who have chronic illnesses or disabilities are thus more likely than other children to be neglected or abused and more likely to enter the child welfare system. This calls for early intervention to support a caretaker's ability to see the baby's strengths, to accept his uniqueness, to foster mutual attachment, and to provide good care.

> Donna N., 19, entered a program for substance-abusing pregnant women when she was five months pregnant. With intensive services, she stopped using alcohol and other drugs. Even so, she gave birth to Daniel in her seventh month of pregnancy.

Daniel was immediately placed in the neonatal intensive care unit (NICU). Ms. N. visited Daniel once, but did not return. The substance abuse program outreach worker visited Ms. N., who confided that the NICU was "scary." The outreach worker offered to go with Ms. N. to visit Daniel. Although Daniel could not be removed from his incubator, the worker taught Ms. N. how to caress Daniel and to talk to him.

When Daniel was removed from the incubator, the worker taught Ms. N. how to hold and rock him, despite the wires and tubes to which he was attached. After nine weeks, Daniel was discharged to home. Two weeks later, Ms. N. called the outreach worker. Daniel had vomited his bottle and was driving her "crazy" with his crying. In anger and frustration, she had shaken him. The worker visited immediately. After providing emotional support to Ms. N., the worker suggested a referral to the local family preservation program. Ms. N. agreed. Intensive services, including counseling for her guilt about Daniel's early birth and referral to an infants and toddlers program, prevented further abuse and enabled the family to stay together.

Early Childhood: Autonomy Versus Shame and Doubt

As with infants, hospitalization is stressful for toddlers. Their wariness of strangers, reliance upon routines and rituals, poor impulse control, and limited ability to verbally communicate thoughts and feelings make it particularly difficult for toddlers to cope with the stresses associated with symptoms, hospitalization, and home care regimens.

Fatigue may limit a child's mobility. Medically necessary physical restraints or restriction of movement, as well as parental worry and overprotection, may frustrate the child's desire to explore and master the environment. Some children with disabling conditions, such as blindness or paralysis, may be unable to explore the environment without assistance.

Thus, depending on the condition, a child's ability to develop autonomy may be compromised by the condition, necessary restrictions, and dependence on others.

Problems of discipline and overprotection may also negatively affect the child's efforts to become autonomous. Sympathy for the child, concern about his or her safety and health, and parental guilt may cause caretakers to treat the child as vulnerable and to become overindulgent and overprotective, leading to increased dependency on the child's part.

Confusion over developmentally appropriate behavior/misbehavior and condition-related behaviors may make it difficult for caregivers to know how to respond to behavior problems. When a child has more than one caregiver, differences of opinions about discipline may lead to conflict. The child may be able to manipulate the caretakers by playing one against the other. Conflict may disrupt family relationships and lead to family breakup. As with infants, toddlers with chronic illnesses or disabilities are vulnerable to abuse.

Play Age: Initiative Versus Guilt

Initiative builds on the autonomy achieved in the previous developmental stage. During this period, the child is better able to separate from parents and caretakers, interacts more with peers, and can distinguish fantasy from reality. Language and expressive skills are generally mastered. The child is a doer, running, exploring, testing new skills, and playing imaginatively.

Chronic health conditions may limit or thwart a child's initiative. Opportunities to develop skills by interacting with peers may be curtailed. The child's cognitive abilities may enable her to understand something of her condition, but misunderstanding may occur. For example, one child with cystic fibrosis misunderstood the word *mucous*. She thought she had mice in her lungs; she worried because lung percussion did not cause the mice to be expelled. Misunderstanding and imagination may create intense fears. Fears of hospital staff who perform invasive or painful procedures may generalize to all adults in medical settings, to all people wearing white clothes, to all men, and so on. A fearful or anxious child may stifle her own initiative. As with toddlers, caregivers may also stifle initiative by treating the child as vulnerable and becoming overly indulgent, overly protective and overly lenient.

School Age: Industry Versus Inferiority

At age 5 or 6, children enter a new world—elementary school. Although they may have been exposed to peers in day care or kindergarten, the size and organization of the school is new. School imposes new demands and expectations.

Industry includes eagerness to build skills and perform meaningful work. The outcome is significantly affected by children's experiences with peers and teachers. Children who succeed and are liked by peers are likely to feel competent and have high self-esteem. Repeated failures foster feelings of inferiority, as does being ignored, disliked, or teased by peers. Children with genetic disorders may miss school because of hospitalizations, medical appointments, and therapies. The child may fall behind in his work and receive poor grades. Fatigue, physical limitations on participation in games and sports, interruptions of the day for medication, or dietary restrictions may isolate the child from peers and lead to teasing. Children schooled at home may have little, if any, peer interaction.

Capable of more complex thinking, the child can compare himself with other children and ask, "Why me?" Stress may result in depressive withdrawal, antisocial behavior, or exaggeration of symptoms as an excuse to remain home. Parental overprotection and lowered expectations may prevent the child from developing autonomy and competence. Struggle over compliance with treatment may emerge as the child strives for autonomy and independence from caregivers.

The impact of genetic disorders on children is quite variable. Some disorders create a visible "differentness" in appearance or behavior that sets a child apart. Rejection by peers may make it difficult for the child to learn social skills. Some conditions, such as mental retardation or mental illness are highly stigmatized in the United States. When out in public, the child may be stared at, commented upon, insulted, avoided, or ignored. The child may internalize feelings of inferiority. Children with visible conditions and their families are likely to begin experiencing the reactions of others as hurtful and exclusionary. Families may experience a wave of grief as the implications of their child's limitations become more socially apparent.

Depending on the specific condition, a child may have multiple service needs, such as physical therapy, occupational therapy, or speech therapy. She may need special resources and devices, such as braces, a wheelchair, special forms of seating, or communication aids. Computers and other technological advances have led to sophisticated but expensive assistive technology. The home may need to be adapted to the child's needs—for example, wheelchair access, fixed location of all objects, or computer access.

The child may need some form of special education, either in a special facility, such as a school for people who are blind, or in special education classes. The child may be pulled out of the regular classroom periodically for special services.

Under federal law, all children with disabilities have the right to appropriate education in the least restrictive setting. Unfortunately, the number and quality of these services vary by school district and state. Even if they have access to such services, parents and caretakers may be unwilling to advocate for the child for fear of alienating teachers, the school principal, or others involved with the child. Some fear that teachers may punish a child for their advocacy.

Parents and other caretakers may treat children with genetic disorders as if they were incapable. They may give the child less responsibility, place fewer limits on his behavior, have increased tolerance for deviant behavior, or indulge his personal whims. It is important that caregivers and significant others view children with genetic disorders as children first, identifying their strengths and abilities to rebound from stressful situations. They must also hold realistic expectations that will enable the children to achieve their optimal potential and satisfying lives. As with younger children, however, caregivers may be overwhelmed by providing for a child with extensive needs, as well as dealing with other problems in living, especially if they do not have adequate supports.

Adolescence: Identity Versus Identity Confusion

Developmental tasks of adolescence include accepting changes associated with physical maturation; integrating changed perceptions of the world in association with the capacity for abstract thinking; coping with intense, fluctuating feelings; building supportive peer relationships; and managing sexuality and sexual activity. In U.S. culture, adolescents are expected to become increasingly independent of their parents. A core theme is identity—creating over time an integrated, autonomous self, equipped for productive work, mutuality, and giving to others. The Eriksonian crisis is identity versus identity confusion.

Adolescence is difficult for many teens. The challenge is greater for those affected by genetic disorders. Integrating physical changes into a positive self-image is difficult for individuals with deformed bodies, delayed puberty, frail appearances, or embarrassing symptoms such as foul-smelling stools or a continually erect penis. The cognitively limited teen may be confused by sexual feelings and not know how to handle them. Unfortunately, adults' reactions may not be helpful. They may misinterpret the adolescent's behavior or respond through their own hang-ups about sex.

> Samuel, 13, who had cerebral palsy, lived in a group home. He began to touch female staff lightly on their breasts. Staff members reacted angrily, telling Samuel that he was "disgusting" and to keep his hands off them. Some staff also punished him by restricting him to his room. A social worker who was a consultant to the group home suggested that Samuel was really seeking connection and suggested that staff arrange for Samuel to have age-appropriate activities with girls. The director of the home contacted the director of a group home for girls. The two planned an ongoing series of joint activities for their residents, including trips and parties. They also had sessions on

dating and how to act towards members of the opposite sex. Samuel stopped touching female staff members.

Adolescents who achieve the capacity for abstract thinking come to a new understanding of the implications of their conditions—for example, that they may die early or be unable to have children. The expression of sexuality and experiencing loving relationships may be impeded if individuals feel they are sexually undesirable, fear being rebuffed, or are ostracized by others.

The adolescent may have intense feelings of depression, anger, loneliness, or despair. Challenging adult authority and developing a sense of self often involves experimenting with drugs, alcohol, sexual activity, and other novel experiences, some of which present a danger to self or others. Risk-taking behavior can be life threatening, such as "forgetting" to take medications or failing to follow special diets.

De facto dependence on others to carry out the activities of daily living or treatment regimens may impede strivings for independence. Autonomy and preparation for adult roles may be problematic, even impossible. Depending on the condition, the individual may have only limited vocational options, be able to work only part time, or be entirely unable to hold a job.

The older adolescent or young adult considering a committed love relationship may be torn between needs for intimacy and fear of burdening the loved one. Depending on the condition, women considering pregnancy may need to consider threats of pregnancy to the well-being of herself and her child. Males and females both have several concerns about having children: the possibility that their children may inherit their disorder, their physical capacity to care for a child, whether they have enough energy to provide adequate love and attention, whether illness-related expenses make it imprudent to take on child-rearing costs, and the impact upon their children if they are hospitalized or die.

Social isolation, inability to fulfill adult roles, and dependence on others are not fertile soil for maturation to adulthood. Because of an especially strong tie and intense involvement in the caretaker role, parents sometimes find it difficult to let go of a young adult with a serious genetic disease. Caring for the child with a chronic illness or disability sometimes becomes the focal point a caregiver's lives. The investment makes it difficult for them to let go. Even so, many adolescents with chronic illness, disabilities, or handicapping conditions take root and thrive. Depending on the person's condition and capacities, vocational training or planning for assisted living in adulthood may be necessary.

Chapter 11

Demands on Caregivers

Raising children is demanding, even under the best of circumstances. Caring for children with serious chronic disorders is even more demanding [Bishop 1993]. Caregivers already under stress due to poverty, other responsibilities, or insufficient coping resources may be unable to provide needed care to children with serious genetic disorders. Fatigue, irritation, frustration, resentment, and other negative feelings may cause them to lash out at children with genetic disorders, whether they are biological parents, relatives, nonrelative foster parents, or adoptive parents.

> Consider the children in your caseload. How many have chronic illnesses or disabling conditions? Select two or three. What care demands are associated with their conditions? How did those care demands contribute to their coming under child welfare supervision?

Caregiver Demands and Family Functions

Families serve many functions—providing economic support, meeting domestic and health care needs, providing opportunities for recreation and socialization, offering affection, and meeting educational and vocational needs [Turnball et al. 1997; Turnball & Turnball 1985]. Each function has associated tasks. Each can be impacted by the presence of a child with a serious genetic disorder.

Economic Needs

Families' economic functions include obtaining income, providing food and shelter, and paying bills. Having a child with special health care needs can increase a family's expenses and, sometimes, reduce income.

Even a family with good health coverage is not protected against all the expenses related to medical care. Suppose, for example, that a child who lives in a rural area far from a major medical center needs to be hospitalized for specialized care. Costs for adults going with the child are likely to include travel, meals, lodging, long-distance phone calls, child care for other children, and loss of work time and income. In addition, the family will be expected to pay any insurance deductible. There may be hidden expenses—such as vitamins, special diets, or special clothing—that insurance does not cover. Costs for some families may include expensive equipment or structural adaptations to the home. Medical expenses may exceed available medical benefits, leaving families thousands of dollars in debt. Parents or other caregivers may feel compelled to obtain an additional job to try to meet expenses.

Income may decrease because of time lost from work. A parent may need to stop working to remain at home to care for the child or may be fired due to time lost from work. Chances for the wage earner to earn more money may be lost because the family needs to remain close to a specialized health care facility or because the wage earner must refuse a promotion because of its added responsibilities.

Family members may be forced to sacrifice dreams and aspirations. They may not be able to afford small luxuries, such as presents for loved ones, birthday parties, baby-sitters, dinners out, or movies. The family may be unable to afford vacations, new furniture, a new home, or college for their children. Family members may experience feelings of loss and depression, and family relationships may be strained.

For low-income families, the situation can be dire.

> Mrs. K., a 59-year-old widow who had immigrated from Nigeria, had assumed care for Isioma, now 8, when Isioma was a baby. Isioma was diagnosed with Williams syndrome. Mrs. K's

daughter, Isioma's mother, was unstable and drug addicted. A doting grandparent who "spoiled" her granddaughter, Mrs. K. was laid off from her job as a night office cleaner. She could not receive her meager Social Security because she was not yet 62. The family's only income was the SSI that Isioma received. Fortunately, Mrs. K. fully her home; she and her husband had worked hard to pay off the mortgage. She was behind on her taxes, however. The gas and electricity had been turned off, so Mrs. K. could not store perishable items, cook, or heat the house. Even though Mrs. K. received food stamps, she usually ran out of food before the end of the month. Isioma's doctor reported Mrs. K. to Child Protective Services for neglect and medical noncompliance, including failure to keep medical appointments. Mrs. K. had to take two buses to get Isioma from her home to the medical center where the child received specialized care. The round trip for both of them cost $5.40, money that Mrs. K. did not have.

Things you can do. Become informed about benefits for which children with genetic disorders may be eligible, including SSI, Medicaid, and food stamps; application procedures for those benefits; needed documentation; and appeals procedures. Inform caregivers of benefits of which they may be unaware. Assist in the application process. Be prepared to advocate on behalf of your client.

Research local branches of service organizations. Determine which will help with transportation, purchases of needed equipment, special medical procedures not covered by health insurance, furniture, and similar expenses.

Contact national organizations concerned with specific disorders of children in your caseload. (See Appendix A.) Do these organizations have state or local chapters in your area? What services do they provide? Will they help cover expenses related to medical care? Can they assist in advocating for recommended services for individual children or adolescents?

Help the child's caregivers develop advocacy skills.

Domestic and Health Care

Meeting the domestic and health care needs of families includes the day-to-day tasks of living: shopping, cooking, cleaning, laundry, transportation, and more. When a child has special health care needs, caregivers must in addition provide or monitor home care regimens and obtain necessary medical, educational, and other needed services. To do so, they must learn

- about the condition and its care requirements;
- new skills, such as using a needle to inject insulin or feeding a child through a tube;
- how to monitor and control symptoms;
- how to judge when a medical crisis is impending and what to do to prevent the crisis;
- skills for documenting the child's needs and advocating on the child's behalf;
- how to build constructive relationships with health, education, and social service professionals;
- how to negotiate health, educational, and social service systems;
- how to normalize their lifestyles and interactions with others; and
- how to deal with their feelings about the child's condition.

Caregivers may find that they can no longer take life's daily routines for granted. For example, a child with diabetes must have a special diet, take insulin, and eat on a schedule that takes into account the timing requirements of insulin and food ingestion. Getting children out of bed and off to school in the mornings can be demanding for any family. With the addition of diabetic procedures, the period before breakfast can become a battleground.

Sleep interruption and fatigue are hardships for many caregivers. For example, asthma attacks usually occur at night. A child with self-injurious, possibly life-threatening behaviors may require 24-hour supervision. Some conditions, such as spina bifida, spinal cord injury, severe mental retardation, and muscular dystrophy may create physical burdens such as lifting, diapering an older child, dressing, hand feeding, giving physical therapy treatments, or doing extra laundry. Asthma, diabetes, phenylketonuria (PKU), cystic fibrosis, and advanced kidney disease require complicated special diets, which may be time-consuming to prepare. Asthma and allergies require extra housecleaning, such as daily mopping of floors and dusting on a continuing basis. Low-income people forced to live in dilapidated housing may find it all but impossible to keep their homes free of dust and allergens.

What you can do. Providing assistance with tasks of daily living may be essential to many families, especially those who are on the margin. Providing a home health worker or housekeeper can be invaluable. It is also important to identify if friends or family members can help out in specific ways, even if it is only by doing the grocery shopping or baby-sitting a couple of hours a week. Some communities also have respite care programs. These programs give caregivers time off by temporarily caring for the child.

Recreation

Optimally, the family provides a setting in which members can relax and be themselves. Families of children with genetic disorders may have to cut back on recreational spending for financial reasons. Travel may be difficult because of the need to transport equipment and supplies. For children with weakened immune systems, it may be unwise to go to places where they may be exposed to the risk of infection. Caregivers may be unable to take a break because they cannot afford or locate baby-sitters or because respite care is not available. Older children's free time may be limited because they have to stand in for adult caregivers.

What you can do. Fortunately, recreational opportunities for children with chronic illnesses and disabilities, many of which have genetic causes, are increasing as a result of mainstreaming and the establishment of special recreational programs and camps. Consider the recreational needs of children and families in your caseload, help families consider how to meet their members' recreational needs, research special programs that may be available in your community and, if necessary, work with others to establish new programs, such as summer camps for children with special health care needs.

Socialization

Many children with disabilities and their families are socially isolated—and social isolation is a risk factor for abuse. Families may encounter obstacles as they attempt to meet the socialization needs of children who have genetic disorders.

Socialization options can be reduced because the child has poor social skills or because community members, neighbors, and relatives have negative attitudes toward "differentness" in a child.

The child may have difficulty engaging with peers because of lack of mobility, impaired verbal and play skills, fatigue, limits on activity, or frequent absence from school. Even when the child approaches peers, he or she may be rejected. Peers may also tease, insult, or even physically assault a vulnerable child.

Caregivers' socialization needs may also go unmet. Relatives, friends, and neighbors may withdraw from the family, often because they are frightened, embarrassed, or don't know how to approach the family. The family may also be unwilling to discuss the child's condition. For example, a parent may be unwilling to upset a grandparent by revealing that a child has a fatal illness. Feelings of social isolation may be intensified if people make hurtful or insensitive comments when the child is out in public. Family members may become reluctant to go outside their home unnecessarily.

Even though socialization opportunities may be few and hard to find for some families, it is important that all family members socialize constructively as much as possible. Fortunately, the current emphasis on family-centered, community-based services has produced many new multiservice programs that include socialization opportunities for the children, adolescents, and caregivers.

What you can do. Understand that families often do not have the time or energy to make contacts that will offer support and relief and that you may need to assume responsibility for developing new contacts for them. Encourage caregivers to teach willing volunteers how to care for the child so that they can have a break. Refer the family to respite care, if available. Locate a family support group, encourage a state genetic support group to

Demands on Caregivers

establish a telephone peer support network for caregivers or for adolescents, and refer the child to activity programs for children with disabilities. Encourage community groups to establish such programs. The Internet provides a means of obtaining information and support for people who are homebound or living in underserved or isolated areas.

Affection

Optimally, families provide their members with unconditional love and fulfill their needs for physical closeness, through touching, hugging, and kissing, for example. Some families are drawn closer together by having a child with special health care needs. Others are driven apart and may even break up. Some families may fail to bond with a child with a genetic disorder, either because of fear the child will die and leave the family or because the child is unresponsive to family members or is physically deformed.

> Suspecting neglect, Dr. V., a hospital pediatrician, referred Faradeh, age 2, to protective services. Faradeh, who was born blind, had been admitted to the hospital for failure to thrive. Faradeh's young mother, Ms. W., complained that, from birth, Faradeh had been "cold," not responding to smiles and other visual stimulation. She also worried that Faradeh might hurt herself if she were allowed to move freely about the environment. Consequently, Ms. W. left Faradeh in her crib all day. She handled Faradeh only for feeding, diaper changing, and bathing. Faradeh was developmentally delayed. Dr. V could find no physical reason for Faradeh's failure to thrive or developmental delay. Dr. V. and the other members of the failure-to-thrive team believed Faradeh's difficulties stemmed from inadequate nurture and stimulation.

As the child matures, issues of sexuality arise. Mentally retarded adolescents, for example, may have sexual urges and be capable of sexual relations but not know how to make appropriate sexual overtures. Depending on their conditions, teens with genetic disorders may need to deal with such issues as sexual rejection by others, infertility, and life-threatening risks of pregnancy. Depression may be expressed in acting-out behavior, including promiscuity. Caregivers may be extremely worried about their teens and sexuality, but feel helpless.

Siblings' needs for affection may also suffer. Caregivers may spend less time with healthy siblings and pay less attention to them. Siblings may miss out on important events of childhood, such as birthday parties and gifts, because their caregivers' time, energy, and resources are not available. Parental or caregiver grief and stress may take away the joy of childhood. Healthy siblings may feel a need to compensate for the child who is ill or disabled. They may assume an inappropriate sense of responsibility and take on caregiving roles and responsibilities. With life-threatening conditions, siblings may fear possible loss of their brother or sister.

The rate of emotional disturbance and behavior problems appears to be higher in siblings of children who are chronically ill or disabled. Unfortunately, helping professionals often overlook siblings' needs and fail to provide potentially valuable support services.

Caregivers' own needs for affection may not be met because of fatigue, time demands, or emotional stress. One common pattern in intact families is for the mother to devote a disproportionate amount of time and energy to the child with special health care needs while the father withdraws from the family.

Sexual issues may also impact on the relationship between biological parents. The cause of a genetic condition may be absorbed into the parental relationship and worsen preexisting problems. The mother of a son with hemophilia, for example, may accept blame, abuse, and accusations from the child's father that she caused their son's illness. Autosomal recessive conditions may intensify doubts and ambivalence about the couple's relationship: "If we had not made love, we would not have had this terrible problem." With intact couples, fear of having another affected child may interfere with sexual relations, perhaps to the point of abstinence. Caregivers' attempts to meet their affectional and sexual needs may lead to affairs.

The situation is particularly complex when a mother's drinking during pregnancy led to fetal alcohol syndrome or fetal alcohol effects. The mother may feel intense guilt; the father, grandparents, and other family members may be angry and bitter.

What you can do. Demonstrate your own acceptance and valuing of the child. One social worker in a genetics clinic remarked that she always found something positive to say about every child, if it was only that the child had "such beautiful fingernails." You can help family members by comfortably accepting a child who is visibly different. If you are uncomfortable and unsure about how to behave at first, you may find that talking about your feelings, rehearsing what you might say and do, and practicing different approaches may increase your comfort and skills. One pitfall is feeling so sorry for a seriously ill, disabled, or handicapped child that you offer pity instead of seeing and supporting strengths. It is important for you to identify your feelings about children with genetic disorders and work to change those that may interfere with your ability to accept a child who is different. (See Chapter 9.)

Encourage family members to identify the positive effects on the family of having a child with a genetic disorder—for example, knowing what is important in life, improved coping skills, understanding differences, or increased empathy for others—even though they would never have chosen this circumstance. Help family members to identify ways in which they can increase closeness. Some families may need to learn how to play together, how to talk with each other, even how to argue constructively. They may also need to learn such basics as how to praise each other and say, "I love you."

Help caregivers understand adolescents' emerging sexuality. Accurate information is important. Try to locate written resources (appropriate for the caregiver's literacy level) or videotapes on sexuality and the child's specific condition. Peer discussion groups for both caregivers and teens can be helpful. If the child or adolescent's specialty care provider has a staff social worker, she or he may be able to work with you in helping family members to better meet their affection and sexual needs.

Educational and Vocational Needs

Meeting a child's educational and vocational needs includes fostering a positive attitude toward school, securing appropriate schooling, developing a work ethic, supervising homework, and obtaining appropriate vocational training. Meeting educational and vocational needs is one of the most demanding caregiving tasks if a child has special educational needs or often misses school due to illness.

The federal Individuals with Disabilities Education Act (IDEA) provides grants to the states for special education and related services for children ages 3 to 5 and for school-age children; requires participating states to furnish a free, appropriate public education to all children with disabilities; and provides grants to states for developing coordinated, comprehensive, statewide networks of early services for infants and toddlers from birth to age 2 who have or are at risk for disabilities [U.S. Department of Education 1992]. Federal legislation also provides grants to states to support vocational rehabilitation services for persons with mental and physical disabilities and their entrance into the regular labor market.

Individuals with disabilities may continue their public education until age 21. Until age 16, each is required to have an individualized education plan (IEP) which is reviewed and revised regularly. When the child reaches age 16, the IEP must be supplemented by an individualized transition plan (ITP). The ITP is a guide to skills needed to make the transition into the community and the work force.

Despite these mandates, not all school systems adequately meet the educational needs of children with disabilities. One reason is that special educational services are expensive. Even with federal support, school budgets may be stretched to provide special education. Goals of individualized education may be short-circuited in smaller school districts by putting children with varied needs into the same classroom. For financially pressed school districts, saving money is an incentive to try to place children in regular classrooms, even when such placements are not in the children's best interests. Needed facilities may not be available in the state, much less locally.

Other obstacles to meeting the educational needs of children with genetic disorders include untrained, insensitive, or overburdened teachers; untrained staff; bureaucratic red tape; and failure to detect a subtle, but serious, problem. Sometimes, a sound plan is made but is not implemented by the classroom teacher.

> Neglected, abused, and abandoned by his alcoholic mother, Richard, 8, entered kinship care when he was 2 years old. He now lives with his grandmother, Mrs. M. At birth, Richard was small for his gestational age, had difficulty sucking, and was irritable. His developmental milestones were delayed. Currently, he is not doing well in school. The teacher describes him as "not paying attention," "hyperactive," and "paying more attention to his peers' business than his own." His grandmother recently reported that she was "fed up" with Richard because he "doesn't mind," "flies off the handle," "fidgets," and is "always running and bumping into things." Despite his history, difficulties with school work and current behavior, Richard has never been evaluated for a possible learning disorder, fetal alcohol effects, or ADHD.

Caregivers often have to educate school personnel about their children's educational needs. This requires understanding of the child's needs, communication skills, and tact. Teachers may resent the underlying implication that they don't know how to teach the child. Parents and caregivers may have to advocate for their children within an often resistant school bureaucracy, and they may worry that staff may retaliate against their children.

In some instances, suing the school may be the only remedy. Unfortunately, many parents and caregivers may be unaware of their children's legal rights and not know that their children are inappropriately placed. They may lack advocacy skills. Their children may languish in inappropriate placements.

Children denied opportunities to learn successfully in school may develop poor self-concepts and low self-esteem. They may become depressed or develop behavioral problems. Unfortunately, schools often blame children and families when children have problems in the classroom; they do not ask if the school is in some way failing the child.

When children under age 3 are at risk for disabilities, they should be referred to an infants and toddlers program for early intervention. Similarly, preschool children with special needs should be referred to the educational system. They may be eligible for appropriate preschool programs.

What you can do. Encourage parents and caregivers to visit their children's schools—on a drop-in basis and by appointment—so they can monitor what is happening in the classroom. If a school-aged child is not doing well in school, assess the climate of the school and specific classrooms. Review the child's educational records to ascertain if an adequate educational or psychological assessment was conducted, if the IEP is adequate, and if the IEP is being implemented as it should be. Similarly, ITPs should be reviewed for youths age 16 or older. Assess whether school personnel need information about the child's condition and guidance about how to manage the child in the classroom. Ensure that such information is provided, if needed.

Assess caregivers' knowledge of the law and, if necessary, teach them about their children's rights under the law. Assess caregivers' readiness and ability to advocate for their children. Identify and contact legal and other organizations that might support advocacy on behalf of a specific child. Inform caregivers about such organizations. Help caregivers prepare for advocacy efforts; be available for consultation and support. If necessary, assume responsibility for advocacy and ensuring that children in your caseload with special educational needs receive the individualized, appropriate educational services to which they are entitled by law.

Objective and Subjective Demands of Care

In assessing a family, considering objective and subjective demands is helpful. *Objective* demands refer to how informed outsiders would rate the overall severity of the demands on caregivers. Most observers would agree that providing round-the-clock home care to a dying child is physically and emotionally demanding.

Subjective demands refer to what caregiving means to the individual parent or caregiver. For example, some biological parents of children with genetic disorders feel guilty. Some blame themselves for causing the child's condition by passing on a faulty gene or chromosome. Others may feel God is punishing them for a previous sin. These emotional costs may compound other caretaking demands.

> Ms. J. felt that the severe mental retardation of her 6-year-old son, Josiah, was God's way of punishing her. When she was 6, Ms. J. had said to her sister, "I wish you were dead." Two days later, her sister was hit by a car and died. Because of her feelings of guilt, Ms. J. indulged Josiah and did not discipline him.

Subjective demand may seem irrational to outsiders.

> A social worker had arranged for a local "grant-a-wish" agency to send Marcy P., a dying child, and her family to Disney World. Three days before the family was scheduled to leave, Mrs. P. telephoned the social worker. She had received airplane tickets for Flight 238. A few years prior, a fortune teller had told Mrs. P. to beware the number 238. Mrs. P. "knew" that if she and her family took that flight, the plane would crash and they would all die. It took almost an hour for the social worker to calm Mrs. P. and to help her consider options, such as asking that the family travel by train.

Even if you think that a caregiver is being irrational, it is important to realize that the subjective burden is real to him or her and should not be dismissed or belittled. Telling people they are being irrational is likely to put them on the defensive. Sometimes, you will be able to offer empathic, helpful, reality-oriented counseling. For example, if Ms. J. was your client, what could you say to her that might be helpful?

Subjective meaning can also help people cope when they can see positive aspects of their situations. Some parents of children with serious genetic disorders, for example, believe that God has chose them to care for their special children because they possess the necessary love and strength. This belief helps carry them through difficult times. Parents who believe they will be reunited with deceased loved ones after death appear able to handle a child's death more easily than parents who do not believe in an afterlife. Sometimes, the most helpful thing a worker can do is help a client change subjective meaning.

> Mrs. W. confided to a social worker that her daughter, Juanita, who was dying of cystic fibrosis, asked her what would happen when she died. Mrs. W. had told Juanita that she wasn't going to die. The worker reminded Mrs. W. that Juanita needed to be able to talk with her about her worries. She suggested that when Juanita raised the subject again, Mrs. W. ask Juanita what worried her. When Mrs. W. did, Juanita said she was worried that she would be all alone in heaven. Mrs. W. told Juanita that she would not be alone. Daddy, Grandpa, and Uncle Pete were in heaven and would be with her. With that, Juanita seemed to relax. Shortly before she died, she told her mother that she was happy that she would be seeing her father again because she missed him. Mrs. W. told the worker about how meaningful it was to her to be able to relieve Juanita's worry.

Serious genetic disorders may place heavy demands on caregivers. Comprehensive assistance calls for a case management approach. Identifying local resources is critical. Today, many communities have agencies or individual social workers who are expert in assisting children and youth with genetic disorders and their families. New communication technologies, such as e-mail and the Internet, are also opening up new opportunities for support, at least for families with access to a computer. Caregivers' needs should be carefully assessed and services provided to enable the family to fulfill its many functions.

Chapter 12
Personal, Social, and Ethical Issues

Issues of genetic information are many and complex and include
- possible stigma;
- possible discrimination in employment or eligibility for insurance on genetic grounds;
- its use in making marital decisions;
- its use in reproductive decision making, including termination of pregnancy for genetic reasons;
- influence on prospective parents' decisions about adopting a particular child;
- confidentiality;
- possible resurgence of the eugenics movement and biological determinism; and
- the belief among some people that genetic services are genocidal.

Genetic Diagnoses

A diagnosis is a label that is used to facilitate detection, categorization, treatment, and prevention of health problems. Genetic diagnoses differ from other medical diagnoses in several ways [Schild 1973]. One is that a genetic diagnosis is familial. It involves and affects nuclear and extended family members, even when they have no contact with each other, as usually occurs when a family member is adopted. Second, a genetic diagnosis changes family members' genetic identity. Third, it impacts upon core issues of sexuality, childbearing, and reproductive decision making.

Genetic Disorders Are Familial

Optimally, a genetic family history includes information about three generations of the nuclear and extended families. Obtaining this information may involve contacting family members to ask questions and, sometimes, to request permission to obtain medical or other records. The requests may touch on sensitive topics, such as incest, mental illness, or suicide. Family members usually cooperate. Sometimes, however, they may be angered by the queries and refuse to cooperate. This may increase family tensions.

A genetic diagnosis may have serious ramifications for family members. They may discover that they have a disorder, even though it had been undiagnosed previously. They may discover they are at risk for a late-onset condition, such as Huntington's disease, or are at risk for having children with a serious genetic disorder. They may need to confront for the first time that they are candidates for genetic services, such as carrier screening or prenatal diagnosis [Omenn et al. 1980].

Although genetic diagnoses often bring nuclear and extended family members closer together, they can also intensify existing family strains and increase alienation. Requests for information from family members need to be handled with tact and sensitivity to family relationships and the meaning of family genetic history to family members.

Genetic Identity

Genetic diagnoses have the potential to stigmatize. They impact upon individuals' genetic identity. Genetic identity refers to a concept of self based on the inherited traits with which we are born [Schild & Black 1984]. It represents the continuity and connectedness of the family, even its immortality.

Serious genetic diagnoses change family and individual genetic identities: "I am a carrier of cystic fibrosis," "We are a sickle cell family," "I passed hemophilia onto my son," or "I may get breast cancer." In their eyes and the eyes of others, the new genetic identity may set the family apart as different from other families. Negative perception of the new genetic identity may intensify preexisting negative self-concepts, low self-esteem, and feelings of worthlessness. Because most genetic conditions are not yet curable, the new genetic identity becomes a fixed attribute of the self, permanent and immutable.

For the biological parents, negative genetic identity may attach to feelings of guilt about the child's disorder. Parents' belief in their goodness as parents may be threatened. The etiology of the child's health problem may be absorbed into the parental relationship and exacerbate preexisting stresses. Autosomal recessive conditions may intensify doubts and ambivalence about the couple's relationship: "If we had not married each other, we would not have this terrible problem." Fear of having another child with a genetic disorder may interfere with sexual relationships.

Fingerpointing may feed into already existing problems within a relationship. The mother of a child with hemophilia, for example, may accept blame, abuse, and accusations from the child's father that she is responsible for their son's disease. If fingerpointing contributes to separation or divorce, the child and issues of his or her care may become embroiled in the parental conflict.

Grandparents may wonder if they transmitted the faulty gene on to the child's parent, blame their child's partner, or accuse the other side of the family ("We never had that in *our* family"). Biological aunts, uncles, and cousins may worry that they are also carrying the faulty gene and that they may pass it on to their children. Siblings may also worry about the chances that they carry the faulty gene and about possibly passing it on to their offspring. In some cases, anxiety is so acute that young adults have themselves sterilized rather than risk giving birth to a child with the familial disorder.

Issues of marriageability may arise, too. Siblings of the affected child may wonder if it is fair to marry someone because of the familial genetic disorder, especially if they know that they are or may be a carrier. Conversely, potential partners may decide to end relationships with individuals who come from families with known genetic disorders.

Social Consequences

The label, "genetic disorder" or "carrier," has the potential for other harmful social consequences, as illustrated by the history of sickle cell legislation. In the United States, sickle cell disease, which occurs in people from malaria zones of Africa and southern Asia, occurs more frequently among African Americans than among any other ethnic group. One in 16 African Americans carries the sickle cell gene; 1 in 600 has the disease.

Partially in response to the civil rights movement, Congress enacted the first sickle cell legislation in 1972. The bill authorized grants and contracts for sickle cell disease services, professional training, public education, and research. The sorry history of the law's implementation included involuntary screenings, confusion of carrying the gene with actually having the disease, confusion of sickle cell disease with communicable diseases, failure to provide follow-up counseling for identified carriers, not protecting confidentiality, imposition of higher medical insurance rates upon carriers, and discrimination against carriers in the military and in civilian employment. Some prominent African Americans charged that the sickle cell program was genocidal [Gary 1974; Reilley 1977; Scott 1970; White 1974].

The history of sickle cell screening programs in the United States points to the sensitivity of genetic information and the need to protect against its abuse. Efforts are under way in Congress to forbid discrimination against people with genetic disorders and their biological families in health insurance and employment [Faden & Kass 1993]. Pressures to reduce health care costs, however, are incentives for employers and insurers to evade any such laws. Some observers are concerned that discrimination against people at genetic risk will continue, whatever its legality. Other concerns are that subtle pressures will be applied to carriers and people with genetic conditions to be sterilized, or that women carrying fetuses with genetic disorders will be pressured to terminate their pregnancies [Garver & Garver 1994].

Another concern is that low-income people will not have access to genetic services. Children and adolescents with genetic disorders may

Personal, Social, and Ethical Issues 115

increasingly be concentrated among the poor. This may intensify stigmas, decrease public support for services for people with genetic disorders and, in the current cost-cutting climate, lead to funding cuts and increasingly inadequate services.

The issue of "genetic labeling" for children is a significant issue for child welfare. One danger is possible stigmatization of children who have a genetic diagnosis or who are from families with an inherited disorder. This may lead to self-fulfilling prophesies and reduce the chances of finding adoptive homes for children eligible for adoption. In addition, courts have upheld complaints of wrongful adoption based upon agencies' failure to inform adoptive parents of genetic disorders within a child's family of origin [Amadio 1989; DeWoody 1993a, 1993b; Freundlich & Peterson 1998; Kopels 1995].

Child welfare workers are ethically responsible for protecting clients' privacy and confidentiality. Balancing the right to privacy against others' right to know is sometimes difficult. In specific cases, you may need to consult with your supervisor—or even a lawyer—about what information to divulge.

Geneticists have also been concerned about issues of privacy and others' right to know in adoptions. One scenario is when an adoptee is diagnosed with a serious genetic disorder. Under what circumstances is the geneticist required to track down biological family member and inform them of the diagnosis? Another scenario is when a serious genetic disorder is diagnosed in a biological family member. Under what circumstances are they required to track down the adoptee?

> Muriel J., who was adopted in infancy, learned that her 4-year-old son had Hunter's syndrome, a X-linked recessive degenerative disease that is fatal in adolescence. The geneticist suggested she contact the agency that handled her adoption so it could notify her biological family. Ms. J's response was, "I don't care about them," and she refused to contact the agency. She did, however, accept referral to a support group. Members of the group also encouraged her to contact the agency. She

eventually did so and authorized her medical geneticist to release information to the agency.

Optimally, genetic diagnoses will be used to secure needed services and help children to achieve their maximum potential. Such a diagnosis may negatively affect a child's self-image, however, and affect outcomes for permanency planning. Further, the diagnosis may lead to insurance and job discrimination against a child and members of his or her biological family. Genetic information must be handled sensitively.

Reproductive Decision Making

Genetic disorders in individuals or families bear on reproductive decision making. Child welfare workers are likely to be involved with four groups of people concerned about their genetic endowment and reproductive issues: adolescents and young adults in their caseloads who have genetic disorders or whose relatives have genetic disorders, graduates of out-of-home care, adult adoptees, and potential adoptive parents.

Advances in genetic technology increasingly give people who are at known genetic risk—and who can afford it—reproductive options never before possible. Genetic services were discussed earlier in this book. Another striking technological development is the availability of alternate paths to conception: artificial insemination by donor, fertilization of donated eggs, and so-called surrogate motherhood. In vitro fertilization, using genetic criteria to select embryos for transplantation, is now in practice. These options are expensive, usually not covered by health insurance, have variable success rates, and are reportedly emotionally trying. Even so, many couples seek them.

These new reproductive options, for the most part, are not available to low-income people. They may not be available to adolescents and young adults under child welfare supervision, at least until they become self-supporting adults. Potential adoptive parents may have tried without success to conceive using reproductive technology. They may still be grieving their inability to conceive and may be ambivalent about adoption. Such issues should be explored fully.

José's teacher referred his mother, Ms. J., to Child Protective Services when José came to school with bruises on his arms and face. When she visited, the CPS worker learned that Ms. J., a department store clerk, became pregnant with José unexpectedly at age 45. Prenatal diagnosis revealed that the fetus had Down syndrome. She attended a parent support group where she was told she would have a "cute, lovable, happy" baby and a son who would be a joy. By age 10, however, José had had multiple medical procedures, including heart surgery. In addition to mental retardation, José has behavioral problems and has been diagnosed with ADHD. Ms. J. believes the support group betrayed her, and refuses to seek further support. Now 55, she is depressed, bitter, and angry at her increasingly difficult-to-manage child.

Many people do not easily understand medical-genetic information they receive. Reproductive risk figures reflect chance and probability. Many people find these concepts difficult to grasp. In addition, many recipients often receive genetic information when they are distraught due to a miscarriage or genetic diagnosis. They may deeply regret decisions made on the basis of poorly understood information.

Terminating Pregnancy for Genetic Reasons

Deciding whether to terminate a pregnancy for genetic reasons is stressful. The parents usually want the child. The process may evoke difficult value dilemmas, such as balancing the well-being of other children in the family against the reluctance to terminate a pregnancy. Other people may pressure a mother or a couple to make specific decisions regardless of personal, religious, or moral values. The couple may disagree about what to do. Sometimes, the decision is in the nature of a gamble—whether to undergo prenatal testing and abort a male fetus with a 50% chance of having a serious, X-linked genetic defect that cannot be diagnosed prenatally (and a 50% chance that the fetus is healthy).

The decision to end a pregnancy is likely to have emotional ramifications for married and unmarried couples, their children, and extended family members. Deciding not to have biological children for genetic reasons can be devastating to couples who want children. Potential grandparents may grieve the loss of grandchildren. There is some evidence that depression and marital disruption are greater after terminating a pregnancy for genetic, rather than psychosocial, reasons [Blumberg et al. 1974] and that children develop behavior problems if their mother terminates a pregnancy for genetic reasons, even if they are not told about it [Furlong & Black 1984].

For people with genetically based reproductive concerns, carrier and prenatal screening may be available, depending on Medicaid and other health insurance coverage in the state of residence. Difficult decisions include whether to give up hope of having biological children or to conceive knowing that the child might have a genetic disorder, whether to obtain prenatal diagnosis if pregnancy occurs, and whether to knowingly give birth to a baby with a genetic condition or to terminate the pregnancy. These decisions are difficult because most genetic disorders are variable and their outcomes unpredictable.

Little systematic research is available about the psychosocial consequences of genetically related reproductive decisions, such as adopting, rather than having biological children. Limited evidence suggests that terminating pregnancy for genetic reasons precipitates crisis; is associated with parental depression and, in some case, psychiatric symptoms; and creates distress for other family members, including children [Black & Furlong 1984; Blumberg et al. 1974; Furlong & Black 1984].

When dealing with clients' genetic concerns, adoption, foster care, and protective services need to be aware of the importance of genetic information to individuals and their families, to their self-concepts, to the reactions of significant others, and to critical life decisions. If referral to a genetic counselor is not feasible, the worker should make every possible effort to connect clients to other reliable sources of information and to ensure their that clients clearly understand the information and its implications for reproductive decision making.

Chapter 13
Cultures, Co-cultures, and Genetics

Many obstacles to mutual understanding between child welfare workers and their clients exist: the involuntary nature of some child welfare services; the impact of oppression upon clients; class, racial, and ethnic distance. We cannot discuss these issues in the space available to us. They are, however, the context of intercultural practice.

If you are not trained in working with oppressed populations, many fine books and social work journal articles are available. Good starting points include issues of CWLA's journal, *Child Welfare,* and two anthologies of journal articles on multicultural issues in social work published by the National Association of Social Workers [Ewalt et al. 1996; Ewalt et al. 1999]. Other CWLA publications include *Cultural Competence: A Guide for Human Service Agencies* and *Culturally Competent Practice: A Series from Children's Voice Magazine.*

This chapter discusses systematic variations that occur across cultures and co-cultures. These variations contribute to mutual misunderstanding between workers and clients. For example, rules of interpersonal communication and eye contact differ. European Americans maintain eye contact during conversation and usually react negatively when conversational partners do not look back, assuming low self-esteem, depression, untrustworthiness, deceit, or disrespect. In some other cultures, eye contact is viewed as invasive, rude, disrespectful, or hostile; people normally look down or to the side.

You can see how easily misunderstandings can occur when two people follow different eye contact norms. The respectful client is thought to be lying; the caring worker is viewed as hostile.

Understanding the dimensions of cultural and co-cultural variation is a potentially valuable tool. Consider the example of eye contact above. Suppose a client isn't looking you in the eye. Knowing that eye contact behaviors vary across cultures, you can ask yourself if your background differs from your client's, if your client might be acting appropriately for her culture, and if you and your client might be misunderstanding each other's eye contact behavior.

> *Knowing how cultures and co-cultures vary, you can ask yourself questions about your clients. The answers can foster mutual understanding and decrease cultural or co-cultural misunderstandings.*

There are three steps toward becoming an effective intercultural worker:
- becoming culturally self-aware,
- developing tools you can use to learn from clients and others about their cultures or co-cultures, and
- being flexible and adapting your practice behaviors to clients' cultures or co-cultures.

This chapter assumes that you are working in the United States, not elsewhere in the world, and that you and most of your clients have dissimilar backgrounds. We begin by defining selected terms. We then present one framework for thinking about cultural and co-cultural variations and comment on its possible application when talking about genetic issues with your clients. We hope this framework will provide tools you can use for future cultural and co-cultural learning.

Terminology

Cultures

One definition of *culture* is *"Learned and shared values, beliefs, and behaviors of a group of interacting people"* [Bennett 1993]. As this definition suggests, differently sized social systems, such as families and workplaces, have cultures. Our focus is *populations*—the inhabitants of a place, country, continent, or other such geographic setting, or a group within a geographic location, such as the *Polish population of Chicago* [The DK Illustrated Oxford Dictionary 1998, p. 634]

Culture is learned. Humans are not born with a culture. Culture learning has many sources: families and other people; objects such as flags, toys, and computers; societal institutions such as schools and religious systems; and mechanisms for passing on history and information, such as storytellers or television. Much cultural learning is unconscious, occurring beyond our awareness. Throughout our lives, the essential messages of our culture are pervasive, repeated, and reinforced [Brislin 1993; Samovar et al. 1998].

Child-rearing practices reveal many ways in which culture is conveyed. In the United States, for example, individual autonomy is highly valued. Most children are asked from a very early age to make decisions about what they want to do and what they prefer. In many other cultures, parents would never ask a child these things. They would simply tell the child what to do.

Cultures are dynamic. They change. People learn new ideas, information, and practices when they are exposed to other cultures. The discovery of new practices, tools, or concepts also induces change. For example, computers and the Internet are creating new vocabularies; generating new experiences, behaviors, and skills; changing some perceptions of the "size" of the world and the "distance" between nations; and fostering new ethical and legal issues.

Co-cultures

Cultures vary internally—this is *intracultural variation*. For example, most U.S. Americans speak English, but with regional (Southern, Mid-Western, New England) and even local (Brooklyn, Baltimore) accents. Intracultural variations are associated with class; gender; religion; ethnicity; geographic region; age; urban, suburban, or rural residency; occupation; deafness; and other factors.

Larger cultures, such as nations, contain smaller subgroups that are distinctive and different in some ways from each other and the larger culture. These are commonly referred to as *subcultures,* but *co-culture* is being used increasingly. The prefix *sub-* connotes *under* or *inferior to; co-* connotes equal validity and also similarities, or sharing, with the dominant culture). A co-culture is a "group of people within a larger sociopolitical structure who share cultural (and often linguistic or dialectical) characteristics which are distinctive enough to distinguish it from the rest of society and from other groups within that society" [Hoopes & Pusch 1997, p. 53].

Examples of U.S. American co-cultures are Amish, African American, Chinese American, Jewish, Chicano, and the military.

We use *co-culture* for populations that live in the United States and share common elements with the dominant European American culture. We use *culture* to refer to culture in general, populations from all parts of the world except the United States, and immigrants to the United States who are not acculturated.

Because genetically there is no such thing as race, we prefer ethnic rather than racial terms, such as African American, European American, and so on.

In the United States, people from different countries are often grouped together by continent—for example, Asian American, Latino, and so on. These are labels imposed in the United States, however, and do not reflect the usually more specific ways in which individuals identify themselves, such as Cuban, Chinese, Iranian, Ethiopian, Cherokee, Hmong, or Ibo.

Lumping people together in broad categories diverts attention away from their unique heritages and may foster stereotyping.

Each person uniquely expresses his or her culture or co-culture. In addition to your region or country of origin, for example, your speech is influenced by such factors as your vocal apparatus (larynx), your gender, the family in which you grew up, and your personality. Friends and family can probably identify you over the phone simply by hearing you say a couple of words. Your voice print is almost as distinctive as your fingerprints. Your style, whether talkative or quiet, vivacious or low-key, is distinctive. When you talk, you add your own stamp to your culture or co-culture.

Culture is like an iceberg. Certain aspects—like language, food, music, or dress—are visible above the water line. Other features are invisible to members of the culture. These invisible aspects of culture include assumptions about the world that we take for granted as the way things are or should be [Paige 1997].

One example is time orientation. Most European Americans think time is important. We divide it into increments of seconds, minutes, hours, and days. We believe it should be used "productively" and not "wasted" and that time is something to be scheduled. Many European Americans are impatient if "kept waiting" and anxious if "running late." People in other cultures don't think about time this way. Talking with someone—maintaining a relationship—may be more important than schedules or being on time. Not all cultures measure time by the clock. Variations in time orientation are a significant area of cultural or co-cultural contrast and misunderstanding [Stewart & Bennett 1991, pp. 73-76].

Most people are unaware of cultural influences upon them. When you and your clients have dissimilar backgrounds, remember that you have many cultural assumptions of which you are unaware. Cultural assumptions influence your perceptions of clients and how you behave with them. For this reason, cultural self-awareness is vital.

Acculturation

One definition of *acculturation* is *cultural change that results from continuous firsthand contact between two groups* [Lustig & Koester 1996]. Child welfare clients differ in the degree of their acculturation into the dominant culture. One factor will be whether they are immigrants or members of traditional U.S. American co-cultures. The latter are already acculturated to some degree and may be bicultural. Immigrants' acculturation, which depends upon many factors, will range from almost none to near assimilation [Kim 1997].

Chances are that the sharpest cultural differences will occur between clients who have immigrated from Latin America, Asia, the Middle East, or Africa and workers who were raised in the United States by parents who were also native-born. Sometimes, workers misjudge an immigrant family's degree of acculturation because its members speak English and have adopted superficial features of the dominant culture, such as dress, food, and behaviors of Western politeness. The family may be retaining deeper, more important aspects of their culture, however, than is apparent.

Workers who have immigrated to the United States may misunderstand clients who are immigrants from other nations, European Americans, or from traditional U.S. co-cultures.

Attribution of Meaning

A key communication concept is *attribution of meaning*. This refers to the notion that we each interpret the world based on our cultural and personal experiences.

> Jot down the word *dog*. Immediately write down the images, words, and feelings that come to mind. How do you think the *meaning* that you attribute to *dog* compares to the meanings attributed by your family and friends? Suppose you met a person from a culture that regards dogs not as pets but as food. How do you think you would react to this? What if that person invited you to dinner? How might that person regard U.S. Americans' indulgences of pet dogs, including "gourmet" pet food and toys?

Every culture has *rule books of meaning*, or ways of viewing and interpreting the world (for example, *dog is pet* or *dog is food*). We do not receive communications passively; we apply our rule books of meaning, actively attributing meaning to the messages we receive.

If you and I apply different rule books of meaning to a message, divergent attributions of meaning may result in misunderstanding and possibly embarrassment, hurt, anger, or offense [Lustig & Koester 1996]. For example, some European Americans, meaning to be friendly, address African

American adults by their first names. African Americans are often angered by this practice, which recalls the etiquette of slavery and Jim Crow, when they had to address European Americans by title and surname while they were addressed by their first names or sometimes with demeaning terms such as *boy*.

> Recall a time when a person misunderstood what you were trying to say. Why did the person misunderstand you? What happened as a result of the misunderstanding? Recall a time when you misunderstood what another person was trying to tell you. Why did this occur? What happened? Might the concept of different rule books of meaning apply to either situation?

Communication

One definition of *communication* is *sharing of meanings*. If two people do not understand a message in the same way, they have not communicated [Lustig & Koester 1996; Samovar et al. 1998].

People often misunderstand each other, even when they know each other well. Mutual understanding is even harder to achieve when people are strangers to each other and come from dissimilar cultural backgrounds. This situation is common in child welfare.

One definition of *intercultural communication* is *a process involving the attribution of meaning between people from different cultures*. This definition does not imply mutual understanding; it highlights that communicators may each attribute dissimilar meanings [Gudykunst & Kim 1997; Lustig & Koester 1996].

Effective intercultural communication occurs when people from different cultural backgrounds achieve shared meanings.

> Think back to a time when you worked with a client with whom you did not share your cultural or co-cultural and with whom you were not successful. At the time, how did you assess the lack of success? Might the problem have been based partly on culturally based differences in attributions of meaning?

Figure 12. Cultural Generalizations

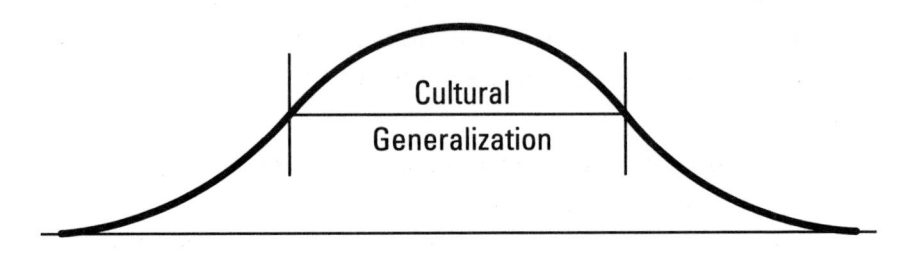

Cultural Generalizations and Stereotypes

Distinguishing between *cultural generalizations* and *stereotypes* is important. A cultural generalization is a statement about members of a culture that is generally true. It is akin to a bell curve, applying most people in the culture, but not all (see Figure 12). The person making the statement

- knows the generalization is not true for all members of the culture;
- is aware that cultures change and that a statement that is correct at one time may be incorrect at another time;
- has an informed basis for the generalization;
- will change the generalization on the basis of new data; and
- in relation to a particular individual, uses the generalization tentatively, as a hypothesis to be explored.

An example of a cultural generalization is, "Most U.S. Americans eat beef." Statistics about the amount of beef consumed per capita document that the statement is true. U.S. Americans vary, however, in the frequency, amount, and type of beef they consume; some do not eat beef for religious reasons or because they are vegetarians.

Thus, a cultural generalization is generally true for most members of the culture; when true, it is not true in the same way for each member of the culture and is untrue for some members.

A *stereotype* is a rigidly applied generalization. It is a fixed, oversimplified image that the holders believe applies to all members of a group. Stereotypes generally resist change, are usually negative, and are often associated with negative feelings towards the group, even hatred. Stereotype holders typically ignore, deny, or explain away information that contradicts the stereotype. "U.S. Americans eat beef" is a stereotype.

> When you encounter a statement about a group, assess whether it is a cultural generalization or a stereotype. In general, cultural generalizations have creditable sources; will be qualified by terms like many, most, or usually; and will note variations and exceptions.

Ethnocentrism

A natural tendency exists for people to be culture-bound, to assume that their values, customs, and behaviors are admirable and right—the way things should be. This is *ethnocentrism*. Ethnocentrism is judging other cultures using one's own cultural norms as standards. It connotes the tendency to view other cultures as inferior. Ethnocentrism is generally unconscious [Samovar et al. 1998].

Ethnocentric child welfare workers may misjudge clients, misread their communications, fail to see cultural or co-cultural strengths and resources, and offer culturally inappropriate services. Clients, too, may also be ethnocentric and look down upon U.S. American ways, including child-rearing practices.

Dimensions of Culture Contrast

If you are ignorant of a client's culture or co-culture, you cannot learn all you might need to know before your first contact. You *can* obtain cultural or co-cultural learning tools to use with your clients. You already have one valuable tool—interviewing skills. You can use these skills to become a cultural learner and to ask culture learning questions. You need only identify when cultural or co-cultural variations may be at work and explore the person's beliefs and practices in specific, relevant areas.

> The guidance counselor at the neighborhood elementary school referred L.C., an 8-year-old Vietnamese boy, to child protective services. L.C. had come to school with what appeared to be

strap marks on the front and back of his body. The CPS worker had cultural interviewing skills. Mr. and Mrs. C. claimed that the marks resulted from treatment for a cold. Knowing that cultures varied in their perceptions of the world, including causes of health problems and the best treatments, the worker asked the parents about their son's symptoms and their treatment. She learned that L. had a cold that they treated with coining, a procedure in which a special oil is applied to the body and a coin rubbed over the body with firm downward strokes. "Coining" is believed to exude the "bad wind" that causes pain, colds, vomiting, and headaches. The worker also learned that L.C. was otherwise well-cared for and that Mrs. C. took L. to a medical doctor when folk remedies did not work. The worker told L.C.'s parents that coining was illegal in the United States. She closed the case, having learned that coining was a meaningful healing practice for many Vietnamese.

Identified areas of culture contrast can help you locate areas of dissimilarity. They can be converted into the question, *"Is there evidence that my and my clients' backgrounds vary on one or more areas of cultural contrast?"* If so, you can ask cultural questions within the identified domain, just as the CPS worker did in the above example. The discussion below includes some examples of cultural learning questions within specific areas.

Stewart and Bennett [1991] identify six dimensions of cultural contrast:
- cultural patterns of perception and thinking,
- language and nonverbal behavior,
- form of activity,
- form of social relations,
- perception of the world, and
- perception of the self.

If a client seems uncomfortable; if his or her behavior seems inappropriate; or if you feel uncomfortable, confused, or irritated, ask yourself if cultural or co-cultural divergence might be present. These six categories can help you locate possible areas of cultural or co-cultural dissimilarity.

Perception and Thinking

Cultures vary in their patterns of perception and thinking. Language, which varies by culture, appears to influence how people think and experience the world. Much of our thinking, of course, occurs in words [Stewart & Bennett 1991].

One way in which language influences perception is variations in vocabulary. In the South Sea Islands, for example, there are numerous words for coconut, which refer to the coconut as an object and also indicate how the coconut is being used. Some languages have words for which there are no English equivalents, and vice versa. Vocabularies also contain words for intangibles. For example, Europeans once believed in the divine right of kings, who were quite powerful. Now, most European monarchies have been abolished and Europeans believe in democracy. Vocabularies thus influence perception by creating categories that direct our attention to certain aspects of our physical, social, and intangible worlds and not others. Vocabularies also influence perceptions because words name categories and concepts. As L.C.'s case illustrates, cultures and co-cultures may have dissimilar categories and concepts [Lustig & Koester 1996; Stewart & Bennett 1991; Samovar et al. 1998].

Language also influences thinking. English grammar tends to foster a search for causes of events and an action orientation. For example, in English we say, "It is raining." The equivalent in some other languages is "Is raining," a descriptive statement with no subject and no implication that an agent (*It*) is causing the rain.

European Americans tend to assume that phenomena have identifiable causes in nature. Their thinking is oriented toward action directed at those causes and positive change. Thinking is focused, goal oriented, and linear. Causes, believed to occur first, are linked to phenomena, which are believed to follow causes. In contrast, Chinese tend to link things that happen at the same time—correlational thinking [Stewart & Bennett 1991].

People in some other cultures don't spend time thinking about how to change things to the same extent as do European Americans and many members of U.S. co-cultures. They believe things happen for reasons they cannot control. They prize acceptance of the status quo, and resignation to one's fate. If they are from a *being* or a *being-in-becoming* culture (see below), they may, in contrast to European Americans, focus attention on the present moment.

Applying the Perception and Thinking Orientation

According to Barna [1997], one of the major stumbling blocks in intercultural communication is the *assumption of similarities*—believing that all humans are basically alike. Do not assume that all people perceive the world and think in the same way. Perception and thinking are areas of cultural contrast. In regard to genetics, you cannot assume that your clients have vocabulary and concepts equivalent to those of biomedicine and genetics. Neither can you assume that they believe genetic disorders are problems that need to be addressed.

> Dr. K. referred the C. family to CPS. The Cs, who were Hmong, had immigrated from Laos a few years earlier and lived in a closely knit Hmong community. Mrs. C. gave birth to a baby with a club foot. Dr. K.'s recommendation of corrective surgery appalled Mr. and Mrs. C. They said that cutting into the foot would anger the spirit that was punishing the family for a sin that an ancestor had committed. The spirit would create even further harm for the family and the baby if surgery occurred. They refused to consent to surgery.

If you were working with the Cs, how might you frame the recommendation for surgery so that it fit within their cultural frame of reference?

Language and Nonverbal Behavior

Language is essential to communication. Cultures differ in interpersonal communication rules, such as the use of talk and silence, persuasion styles, nonverbal behavior, and simplicity versus ornamentation of speech. Even when communicators are speaking the same language, different communication rules may foster misunderstanding and even conflict.

> **Nonverbal Communication Behaviors**
> - *Interpersonal space:* the distance between people who are communicating
> - *Interpersonal touch:* the degree to which one person touches another, the type of touch, its location on the body, its duration, its strength, and its intention (loving, friendly, hostile)
> - *Posture:* leaning forward or backward, open or closed, relaxed or stiff
> - *Body orientation:* away or toward the other person
> - *Hand gestures:* frequency, distance from the body, degree and direction of movement, expressive or inexpressive
> - *Gaze:* looks up, looks down, looks to side, intensity, circumstances in which gaze changes
> - *Eye contact:* frequent or infrequent, circumstances in which eye contact does or does not occur
> - *Facial expressions:* expressive or inexpressive, degree and circumstances of smiling
> - *Speech:* volume, speed, frequency, and duration of silent periods; circumstances in which speech and silence occur

Nonverbal Communication

Cultures and co-cultures vary in the specific nonverbal communication behaviors they use and the meanings attributed to them, as illustrated in the earlier discussion of eye contact. The box above lists some components of nonverbal communication behaviors that vary among cultures. Exercise 8 on page 153 suggests ways to heighten your awareness of communication behaviors.

Low versus High Context Communication

Cultures and co-cultures vary in their orientation of *low context communication* versus *high context communication* (LCC/HCC). LCC and HCC are not opposites; they are end points on a continuum. Different cultures and co-cultures are at different points along the continuum. The degree of LCC/HCC differs by setting. For example, most European Americans, usually LCC, are HCC when at home with their families. LCC and HCC people often misunderstand each other.

LCC people are direct. They say what they mean. Their comments are pertinent to the topic, clear, concise, and well-organized. They are unreserved, willing to reveal personal information. LCC is *sender-oriented;* senders are responsible for transmitting messages clearly and understandably [Gudykunst 1994; Stewart & Bennett 1991].

LCC people perceive nonverbal behaviors as comments on verbal messages, not as messages themselves. Thus, voice tone and facial expressions reinforce or modify meaning of the words used—for example, "That's *great"* can be true ("That's wonderful") or sarcastic ("That's terrible"). LCC individuals attend to the verbal message primarily.

High context communication, on the other hand, is indirect, implicit, and ambiguous. HCC people communicate in ways that maintain group harmony. HCC individuals are pleasant and polite and avoid saying anything that might embarrass, shame, or anger others. Rather than speaking directly, they may use analogies, metaphors, or stories to make a point. Personal information usually is not shared. HCC is *recipient-oriented;* the person who receives the message is expected to infer the meaning and realize, for instance, that "That's an interesting idea" means "No" [Gudykunst & Kim 1997; Yum 1997]. Japan is an example of a HCC culture.

HCC individuals attend to the communication *context*. Meaning may be signaled by the setting, by slight variations in courtesy behaviors, by who is or is not present, by a slightly prolonged silence, or by what is not said. HCC people usually are empathic. They are skilled at recognizing and reading clues [Gudykunst & Kim 1997].

Because they attend to words, not context, European Americans often misread high context communication. They may feel confused or frustrated and think the other person is wasting time or talking in circles. They may assume an agreement has been reached when it has not and become irritated when follow-through on a supposed agreement does not occur.

HCCs often feel that LCCs are rude, even insulting [Gudykunst & Kim 1997].

Assuming you are an LCC person, have you ever had a client who seemed to talk in circles and who left you feeling confused and frustrated? How did you explain to yourself what was happening at the time? Looking back, were you and your client perhaps located at different points along the low-high context communication continuum?

Applying the Language and Nonverbal Orientation

Communication norms include what can and cannot be discussed and with whom. Genetic family histories and genetic disorders are sensitive and possibly taboo topics. Tact is required, especially when working with clients of diverse cultural or co-cultural backgrounds. Clients may believe that talking about a child's health problem will bring bad luck, think you are rude for asking personal questions, or feel that you are shaming their families. Before asking about child or family health, ask if the family's culture permits such discussion. Attend carefully to the person's response. An HCC person may conceal anger or embarrassment by politely agreeing and smiling. If a client avoids questions or gives answers that don't make sense to you, she of he may be an HCC individual who expects you to understand the answer is no. Such interviewing skills as checking your understanding of clients' messages and obtaining feedback about clients' understanding of what you have said are essential in intercultural interviewing.

Form of Activity

Activity orientation defines a culture's view of human action. Three categories are *being-in-becoming, being,* and *doing. Being-in-becoming* is oriented toward developing the whole self into an integrated whole. It is often present in cultures that place primary value on spiritual life. One example of being-in-becoming is Zen Buddhist monks, who spend their lives in contemplation and meditation to fully develop the self [Stewart & Bennett 1991; Lustig & Koester 1996; Samovar et al. 1998; Kluckhohn & Strodtbeck 1961].

Being refers to spontaneous activity and living in the moment. Many Latinos, for example, take great delight in talking with family and friends for hours, believing that being in the present moment is one of the joys of life. Some *being* cultures are also characterized by acceptance of the status quo, often because of a view that fate or other powers control events [Stewart & Bennett 1991; Lustig & Koester 1996; Samovar et al. 1998].

European Americans' orientation is *doing*. To them, change is natural and good. They believe they can control their own lives. Activity is purposeful and planned and has identifiable outcomes. Closely related is an emphasis on identifying problems and problem solving. [Kohls 1988; Stewart & Bennett 1991; Lustig & Koester, 1996].

You, a child welfare worker, are a problem solver. Chances are you are on a different wavelength than members of being-in-becoming and being cultures, who may prize patience, acceptance, and resignation. Unfortunately, clients' beliefs that they cannot influence what happens are often reinforced by life experiences, including encounters with unresponsive health and human service systems.

Applying the Form of Activity Orientation

Some clients may believe nothing can be done about genetic disorders. They may not see the point of a family genetic history or of complying with treatment recommendations. Theirs is a fatalistic, passive orientation, not an active one. If serious risk to a child's health exists, and you cannot influence the client, a cultural or co-cultural mediator may be able to persuade the client to obtain recommended medical treatment and other services. If the mediator fails, you will need to judge whether legal action for medical neglect may be necessary. If you decide legal action is necessary, you will, of course, be imposing your values and disempowering the child's caretakers. Such actions should not be taken without strong reason for believing the child will be harmed if you do not act.

Forms of Social Relations

The social relations orientation describes how people organize themselves and relate to each other.

Individualism versus Collectivism

Individualism and *collectivism* are two common forms of social relations. They, too, are end points of a continuum, not opposites. Individualistic societies value the individual over the group; collectivist societies value the group over the individual. The United States is perhaps the most individualistic nation in the world.

European Americans consider individuals as the primary units of society. They value self-reliance, autonomy, and independence. Individuals strive for individual achievement, material success, and self-fulfillment. When communicating, individuals are expected to share their beliefs, feelings, opinions, and personal information. Individuals make decisions about matters that affect their lives. Competition is seen as a social good. Interpersonal conflict is viewed as normal and is addressed directly [Andersen 1997; Gudykunst & Kim 1997; Lustig & Koester 1996; Gudykunst 1994].

Collectivist cultures want individuals to fit into the group. Ingroups are usually sharply differentiated from outgroups. Collectivist cultures emphasize the goals, needs, and views of the ingroup over those of the individual; the social norms of the ingroup rather than individual pleasure; shared, rather than unique, beliefs; cooperation rather than individual achievement. The goal of communication is group harmony. People are polite and respectful and suppress their own feelings and views. Conflict is avoided; when it occurs, it is handled indirectly, perhaps by a third party. Collectivist cultures tend to predominate in Africa, Asia, Latin America, and the Middle East. Worldwide, the extreme individualism of the United States is in a minority [Andersen 1997; Gudykunst & Kim 1997; Lustig & Koester 1996; Gudykunst 1994].

Family

Family structure tends to vary in individualistic and collectivistic cultures. In individualistic cultures, several types of nuclear families (married two-parent, single-parent, step, and so on), couples, and single individuals are the norm. Families are expected to be self-supporting and to live in their own quarters, often far from relatives. In collectivist cultures, extended families, which may include great-uncles and aunts, third cousins, and even more distant relatives, are characteristic. Family members may live in the same residence or compound, eat together, share financial and other resources, cooperate in household tasks, and have well-delineated reciprocal obligations. Some extended families have fictive kin, people who are considered family but are unrelated by blood or marriage [Andersen 1997; Gudykunst & Kim 1997; Lustig & Koester 1996; Gudykunst 1994].

Decision Making

European Americans expect biological parents or legal guardians to make decisions affecting their children. They also expect older children and adolescents to participate in decisions that affect them. In collectivist cultures, decision making authority may lie elsewhere in the family—for example, among several adults or with a patriarch. Extended family members may believe they have the obligation and right to meet with you. They may believe you should share information about the child and biological parents with them, which is counter to the child welfare norm—and law—of confidentiality. Children and adolescents may be seen as too young to be involved in decisions.

Families also vary on other dimensions. One is high versus low context communication, which we discussed earlier. Others include direct versus indirect conflict resolution strategies, power distribution (equality versus inequality), and sex role norms. European American families are relatively egalitarian. In contrast, inequality in power and status is the norm in some collectivist cultures. Families may be authoritarian. Submission to authority may be highly valued. [Andersen 1997; Gudykunst & Kim 1997; Lustig & Koester 1996; Gudykunst 1994].

Gender roles may be unequal. In individualistic cultures, such as the United States, men and women are relatively equal. Collectivistic cultures tend toward sharper gender role differentiation and greater inequality. Males may be considered as superior to women and wield authority over wives and children. Males may also be responsible for contacts with external systems, such as hospitals and schools. In some cultures, men and women do not talk with the opposite sex if they are not members of the same family. Family members, including women, may not accept women in positions of authority, such as doctors and social workers. European Americans are usually amazed to discover that people from some other cultures accept—and value—inequality and that members of subordinate groups, such as women, regard submissiveness as a virtue.

Application of the Social Relations Orientation

Your efforts to change a situation may come to naught when working with collectivist families if you do not include family decision makers and respect family norms. Several family members may come to a planned genetic family history interview. They may expect to participate in decisions to accept a referral to a genetic service or to comply with recommended treatment and services. In some collectivist families, it may be inappropriate for you to talk with children, adolescents, young adults, or women. It may be appropriate to address only men, elders, or a patriarch.

If you are a woman assigned to a family with strong male authority, reassigning the case to a male worker is recommended. If that is not possible, consider recruiting a male to work with you, preferably one who is familiar with the client's culture and who will be respected by family members.

Culture Learning Questions: Family

The following questions may help you to learn about the families characteristics and decide how to adapt your practice to families' cultures.

Try to ask culture learning questions with a relaxed, interested, conversational manner. Use your basic attending skills to follow what your client-teacher is telling you and deepen your learning. People often start to tell about things about which you never thought to ask but which are highly relevant. Use planned culture learning questions as a guide, not as a rigid outline. Don't fall into the trap of asking too many closed questions and seeming to grill the client.

- Who belongs to the family?
- Where do family members live?
- Who represents the family in its contacts with the outside world?

- How are decisions made? Who needs to be consulted? Who makes the final decision? What happens if family members disagree about an important decision?
- Are men and women allowed to talk with members of the opposite sex?
- Is obedience important to you? Do you expect children to obey you? Other adults? Should wives obey their husband? Should adult children obey their parents? What happens if someone is disobedient?
- Do men and women in your culture talk together about sexual issues, pregnancy, and birth? Are these topics we can discuss?
- Do people in the United States often do things that you think are rude or disrespectful? What kinds of rude and disrespectful things do they do?
- Are there courtesy behaviors I should be aware of? Are there things I should do to show proper respect for family members?

Perception of the World

Perception of the world refers to how people perceive and evaluate the world and how they explain phenomena.

World View

Cultures have world views that influence perception, beliefs, and values. They address the spiritual world, nature, human nature, existence, the universe and cosmos, life, death, and other philosophical issues. European American culture views humans as distinct from nature and other forms of life. It regards nature as something to be manipulated and controlled, as exemplified by the Human Genome Project [Kluckhohn & Strodtbeck 1961; Stewart & Bennett 1991; Samovar et al. 1998].

Most European Americans view the physical and spiritual worlds as separate. Not all cultures make this distinction. One view, for example, stresses spiritual unity among all forms of life and inanimate objects. This view fosters a sense of connectedness to the external world. Another view is that nature is dangerous and animated by spirits. This fosters an attitude of helplessness in the face of nature [Stewart & Bennett 1991].

Health Beliefs and Practices

Different perceptions of the relation between humans and the world are expressed in attitudes towards health, the body, and the causes of disease. Western health practices are firmly rooted in the concept of the body as a biological mechanism that is susceptible to invasion by external agents (bacteria, viruses), to unfavorable environmental conditions (asbestos, poor sanitation), and to poor diet [Stewart & Bennett 1991].

Other cultures explain disease and disability differently. Health beliefs can be divided into three categories: biomedical, personalistic, and naturalistic [Samovar et al. 1998].

- **Biomedical.** This is the dominant view in the United States. Disease and disabilities are the result of abnormalities in the body's functioning or structure. These are viewed as caused by physical agents such as bacteria and viruses or by physical conditions such as injury or aging.
- **Personalistic.** Disease and disability are viewed as caused by a supernatural being (deity or god), nonhuman being (ghost or evil spirit), or a human (witch or sorcerer).
- **Naturalistic.** The body is believed to contain certain humors, substances, or principles that need to be in balance. Health problems result from imbalance of the body's elements, such as hot and cold, or yin and yang.

Treatment may be provided by nonmedical healers, such as *shamans* or *curanderos*, who may be viewed as spiritual agents. Treatments include herbal remedies, coining, superficial burning in specific locations, cupping, pinching, incantation, and myriad other folk remedies [Boyle & Andrews 1989; Lecca et al. 1998].

In some cultures, people avoid talking about health problems, believing that such talk brings bad luck. In the United States, users of folk health practices often conceal them from members of the dominant culture. Beliefs and practices may not be volunteered; you may need to ask.

Application of the Perception of the World Orientation

You cannot assume that others see illnesses and disabilities as you do. Your clients may not accept biomedicine. They may have alternate ideas about how diseases are caused, such as the "evil eye" or even as a blessing from a god. They may use folk remedies. Many combine folk practices with Western medical care. When a child is ill, you should always ask if an over-the-counter or prescription medicine is being used with a folk remedy. Drug and treatment interactions can be harmful, even fatal.

Ascertain clients' health beliefs before introducing genetic topics. They may not have concepts equivalent to those of genetics. They may find some ideas, such as genes, difficult to understand, unbelievable, even laughable. If clients are not amenable to biomedicine, try to frame your presentations so that they fit with clients' health beliefs. For example, a faulty gene could be presented as possibly the effect of a curse. Respect your clients' beliefs; do not label them negatively as nonsense or superstition.

Culture Questions: Health

Following are some possible culture learning questions about health. They are adapted from those of Samovar, Porter, and Stefani [1998].

- I would like to talk with you about ———— health problem(s). I know some people don't talk about health problems because they may believe that talking about such things brings bad luck. What about you? Is talking about health problems okay with you?
  If the person indicates that talking about the problems brings bad luck or could harm someone, ask if the reason for talking changes the luck, or if bad luck or harm can be undone. Continue only if the person feels safe, unless the risk to the child is severe.
- What do you call the condition?
- Why do you think it started when it did?
- What do you think the condition does to your child?
- How does it work?
- How severe is the condition? Will it last for a long or short time?
- What kind of treatment should your child receive? Who should provide the treatment?

- What are the most important results you hope your child will get from treatment?
- What are the chief problems that the condition has caused for your child? For you?
- What do you fear most about the condition?

The questions can be planned and used when asking about genetic family histories or a child's health. They can also be used spontaneously, when a person refers to a health condition or treatment during an interview. The important thing is that you adopt the role of *culture learner;* your client or another culture member becomes your teacher.

Perception of the Self

I-self

Self-orientation describes the nature of the self and the personal qualities that are valued and respected. European Americans believe the self is located solely within the individual, is unique, and is separate from other selves. Their self-orientation combines with the doing pattern to create the belief that people can improve themselves and control their fates. European Americans have an *I-self.* They give priority to personal preferences, opinions, choices, and creativity. Individuals are viewed as independent, self-reliant, and responsible for decisions that affect their lives. Child-rearing practices support the development of the autonomous self, from having infants sleep alone to expecting young adults to live independently and support themselves [Stewart & Bennett 1991; Roland 1994].

Familial-self and We-self

The I-self of Europe and North America contrasts with the *familial self* of most of the rest of the world. Most cultures stress dependency, interdependency, receptivity to others, and reciprocity. One aspect of the familial self is the *we-self.* The experience of self varies from relationship to relationship. The inner images of self and others are more closely connected than in I-selves. The we-self also has more permeable emotional boundaries between the individual and other people. Esteem is experienced in a we-self context and is related to the reputation of the family. An inner attitude of receptiveness and openness to constant guidance from others is also characteristic.

Child-rearing practices support the development of the interdependent self, from having infants and toddlers sleep with their parents or other adults to expecting young adults to remain at home and to accept family decisions that affect their lives—for example, selection of a spouse [Lustig & Koester 1996; Stewart & Bennett 1991; Roland 1994]. People with I-selves often find it difficult to understand people who have familial-selves. They find it hard to believe that familial-self individuals do not envy individual freedom, independence, and autonomy and that they sometimes look down on I-self people as shallow, selfish, and irresponsible.

Implications of Different Perceptions of the Self

Genetic disorders are familial and affect all family members. The familial impact is likely to be even greater for people from familial-self cultures. First, depending on the cultural health belief system, the cause may be perceived as familial—for instance, that the birth of a child with a birth defect is a family punishment for a sin committed by an ancestor. Secondly, feelings of family shame may be strong. Too, the child's disorder may be considered as a private family matter that should not be revealed outside the family. Finally, the family may expect to care for child completely, without outside assistance. Seeing a child welfare worker may be completely foreign to the family's experience and culture.

Familial-self families' expectations of a child with a serious illness or disability may differ from those in I-self cultures, particularly in the United States. The I-self culture's stress on individual autonomy and achievement is expressed in services—such as infant stimulation, occupational therapy, and special education—intended to enable children with special health care needs to achieve their maximum potential. That is, they are expected to improve themselves.

Members of we-self cultures may not view dependence as a problem, nor independence as a goal. They may see it as natural for the family to care for and even indulge the child with a serious illness or disability, even in adulthood. They may view negatively expectations to increase such children's capabilities, as a burden on the children and a failure to accept and love them. They may disapprove of such programs as the Special Olympics, seeing them as putting children's impairments on display and embarrassing children and their families.

Traditional cultural practices toward infants with birth defects will shape immigrant families' attitudes. Some other cultures' practices differ markedly from those in the United States. In China, for example, newborns with birth defects (and sometimes girls) are still left to die.

The United States is the wealthiest nation in the world. It has highly advanced medical technology. Sometimes, hundreds of thousands of dollars are spent on keeping a single prematurely born baby alive. One of the reasons for the increasing numbers of children with special health care needs in the United States is medicine's ability to prolong the lives of children who once would have died in infancy, childhood, or adolescence.

Place yourself for a moment in the position of a person from an impoverished country. Suppose it is common for children to die from premature birth, diarrhea, malnutrition, or famine. If you had to choose between feeding a healthy child or a child with a severe health problem, which would you choose? How might you view U.S. practices? What if you believed that you have to accept fate, that one should not interfere with God's will, or that the child's birth is the family's punishment for an ancestor's sin? What if your culture taught you resignation and acceptance?

> When she was pregnant, Ms. G., 37, learned that her baby had a brain hernia and that brain tissue was leaking through the opening. The physicians told her that the baby would not survive and recommended abortion. A childless, devout Roman Catholic, Ms. G. decided to have the baby. Much to everyone's surprise, the baby, Lucia, was able to breathe on her own and survived. Lacking a cerebral cortex, she had no other capacities, not even the ability to suck or swallow. Ms. G. fed her through a tube inserted into her stomach. She enrolled Lucia in a daily infant stimulation program. At six months, Lucia had brain surgery due to leaking spinal fluid.

Ms. G. had immigrated with her family from El Salvador when she was 29 years old. Her family asserted that Lucia's birth defect was God's will and punishment for having a baby out of wedlock. When they visited, they refused to acknowledge the baby's existence. The baby's father, Mr. I., had immigrated from Ethiopia. He was visiting Ethiopia, then in the midst of famine, when Lucia was born. When he returned, he was appalled that Lucia was kept alive, fed through a tube, and attending an infant stimulation program. He refused to see the baby and broke off with Ms. G. Lucia died of pneumonia at 13 months.

Culture Learning Questions: I-self, Familial-self, and Child Care

Cultures' perceptions of the self influence child-rearing practices. The following questions focus on aspects of caring for children with genetic disorders. Remember not to grill your clients about their cultures or co-cultures. Think of yourself as a learner and your client as a cultural teacher.

- What kind of adults do you want your children to become? What are your hopes for (child with genetic disorder)?
- How do you help your children grow up to be good adults? What about (child with genetic disorder)?
- What are some things your children have done that make you proud of them? What about (child with genetic disorder)? Did you let them know you were pleased? How? (Note: In China and some other cultures, parents avoid saying good things about children because the gods might want good children. The custom is to complain and say negative things about children so the gods will not take them away.)
- What are some things that your children have done for which they had to be punished? What about (child with genetic disorder)? Who punishes the children? How?
- When your family gets together, does (child with genetic disorder) join you? What do the other children do? Does (child with genetic disorder) participate? How do other family members treat (child with genetic disorder)?

- Who helps you raise your children? Who participates in caring for (child with genetic disorder)?
- Who contributes to paying the extra costs of raising (child with genetic disorder)?
- Who participates in making decisions about your children? Who participates in making decisions about the treatment and education of (child with genetic disorder)?
- Some people believe problems should be handled within the family and that the family should not go to outsiders for help. Some families are shamed if a problem becomes known to outsiders. What about your family?
- What do family members think caused (child with genetic disorders)'s problem? What about you? Do you agree with them?
- If (child with genetic disorder) has to go to the hospital, who goes to the hospital with the child? Who meets with the doctors? Who speaks to the doctors? Does it make a difference if the doctor is a woman?
- Some people go to medical doctors but are helped also by other healers. What about you? Who is treating your child? What kinds of treatment are you getting for (child with genetic disorder)? Are you giving your child medicines prescribed by the doctor and remedies provided by a healer? What are they? Have you told a doctor or nurse about all of your child's treatments? Are you aware that they sometimes cancel out each other's effects?
- What services have been offered to (child with genetic disorders)? Which have you accepted? How do you and members of the family feel about the services? Are they helpful or are they a burden on (child with genetic disorder)? Do they make his or her life harder or easier?
- What do you think should be done for (child with genetic disorder)?

Being Interculturally Competent

Becoming an interculturally competent communicator takes time and effort. It may be uncomfortable sometimes. Although formal training in diversity practice is widely available, you have to be a self-directed learner.

We conclude this chapter with suggestions for your growth toward intercultural competence.

Know Yourself

What you bring to your meetings with clients influences what happens. Cultural self-awareness is vital. Fortunately, there are many paths to cultural self-awareness. Perhaps the best is to take advantage of and create opportunities to interact with diverse groups of people. Contact with diversity will heighten your awareness of your own culture. You can also ask them how they see you and U.S. American culture.

Another path is reading descriptions of your native culture or coculture and identifying ways in which the descriptions fit and do not fit you. *Distant Mirrors: America as a Foreign Culture* [DeVita & Armstrong 1993] is a fun book for persons born and raised in the United States. It is a brief collection of essays written by anthropologists visiting the United States, some of them on amusing topics.

Knowing *your attitudes toward members of various groups is also important.* Exercise 9 on page 154 will quickly orient you to your intercultural history. Exercise 10 on page 156 has questions to consider.

Skills

Knowing How to Gather Information

You can obtain cultural knowledge in various ways. Earlier, we mentioned becoming a cultural learner and asking culture questions. We gave examples of possible culture learning questions within three of Stewart and Bennett's [1991] areas of cultural contrast. Another tool is observation. Opportunities to observe in our daily lives abound. For example, we can observe parent-child interaction in supermarkets, on playgrounds and in agency offices. You can also observe people on the street; in ethnic neighborhood markets; at ethnic events; or if you are fortunate enough to travel, in other regions of the United States or in other countries.

Other culture learning activities include

- traveling outside the United States, avoiding tourist areas, and seeking opportunities to interact with members of the host culture;

- seeking out and talking with people of different cultural and co-cultural backgrounds in your neighborhood, workplace, and other locations;
- viewing foreign movies;
- reading novels, autobiographies, and biographies dealing with people from diverse backgrounds;
- reading summary descriptions of various cultures, such as those in some social work and child welfare texts;
- studying a language; or
- attending in-service training sessions, continuing education, and professional conferences focused on intercultural practice.

Focus your learning in areas relevant to your practice. If you work in adoption, you might want to learn about cultural or co-cultural adoption practices, such as the informal adoptions that occur in African American communities or, in some other cultures, gifts of children to childless couples. If you are with child protective services, looking into how children are punished, for what, and by whom is relevant.

> With what kinds of situations do you work on a daily basis? What values do you apply? What knowledge? If you could learn only three things about a culture or co-culture, what would they be? What sources could you use to obtain this information? Within your general topic, what specific questions might you ask?

Culturally and Co-culturally Congruent Behaviors

The effectiveness of intercultural communication requires behavioral flexibility and ability to adapt our behaviors to our clients' cultures and co-cultures. Optimally, if we are not bilingual, we will learn to speak another language, or at least a few phrases. At a minimum, we should modify our courtesy behaviors. To the degree possible, comments should be descriptive, nonevaluative, and nonjudgmental, remembering that what seems wrong to us might be correct in the client's culture [Gudykunst & Kim 1997; Lustig & Koester 1996; Samovar et al. 1998].

Using an Interpreter

If at all possible, use professional interpreters when meeting with people who do not speak languages in which you are fluent. Meet the interpreter before the interview to review its purpose, the probable topics, and words and concepts that may be difficult to translate. Culturally informed interpreters should be able to tell you about courtesy and status recognition behaviors, male-female communication, and impolite or taboo topics. Culturally informed interpreters may also be able to offer guidance on how to approach potentially problematic topics.

Avoid using friends and family member as interpreters. They may edit clients' comments to you. Friends and family members may also want to provide their own views or seek to protect your clients by screening and changing what you say. Many clients will not speak freely in front of family, friends, and community members. Many men and women will not talk about sexual or other intimate matters in the presence of the opposite sex. Particularly avoid using children and adolescents as interpreters. Using younger family members to interpret for older family members may shame the older person and disrupt the usual balance of child dependence and adult authority.

The actual style of interviewing through interpreters depends upon interpreters' training and skill, your and your client's comfort, and the setting. Chances are you will use consecutive rather than simultaneous interpretation. If so, speak slowly and clearly, in short units of speech. Avoid long, complex questions, statements, and discussions. Here are some other tips:

- Begin the interview with some casual talk and warm-up questions to create a climate of ease and trust.
- Plan for more interview time that usual, as an interpreted interview takes longer.
- If acceptable within the client's culture, look and talk directly to the client; do not look at or talk to the interpreter.
- Address the client in the second person. (How long have you been in the United States?) Do not use the third person. (How long has she been in the United States?)

- Encourage the interpreter to translate the client's own words and to avoid paraphrasing or summarizing.
- Pay attention to the client's nonverbal behavior. Nonverbal communication norms vary; be alert to discrepancies between the client's nonverbal behavior and what the interpreter is saying.
- Maintain an engaged interaction with the client.
- Be patient [Rauch et al. 1993].

Personal Qualities

Mindfulness

Mindfulness is important to intercultural practice. It is paying attention. We need to be mindful of our communication behaviors and that clients' attributions may not be the same as ours. We need also to keep in mind that clients' communication norms may differ from ours. We may misunderstand what a client is attempting to convey and vice versa. When mindful, we provide feedback to clients about how we are interpreting their messages. Similarly, we request feedback about their understanding of our communications to them. Mindfulness helps us listen more effectively [Gudykunst & Kim 1997].

Tolerance for Ambiguity

Also valuable is tolerance for ambiguity—the ability to function in unclear, uncertain situations. People who have low tolerance for ambiguity tend to jump to conclusions and select information that supports their beliefs. People who have high tolerance for ambiguity seek further, objective information before forming impressions. Your first reactions to a family situation may be based on misunderstanding or ethnocentrism. Hold off on forming opinions until you have explored whether specific behaviors or practices are common or acceptable within the family's culture [Gudykunst & Kim 1997]. If a cultural practice is not usual, accepted, or legal in the United States, educating the client may be sufficient, and further action unnecessary.

Ability to Empathize

Empathy is being able to see from another's point of view. It involves careful listening and showing concern, seriousness, and interest. Barriers to empathy include ethnocentrism, holding stereotypes, jumping to conclusions, and disinterest in understanding the person. Ways to increase intercultural empathy are learning about clients' cultures, cultural questioning, and resisting the tendency to interpret the other's communications and actions from your cultural point of view [Gudykunst & Kim 1997; Samovar et al. 1998].

European Americans tend to assume that emotions are natural and universal and that empathy is feeling with the other person [Green 1999]. We cannot assume, however, that all people react emotionally in the same way or that they have the same rules for displaying emotion. For example, high context communicators often conceal their emotions in the interest of social harmony. Green suggests that the more remote the client's culture and experiences are from the worker's, the greater the possibility for distortion and misunderstanding of emotional signals. He recommends that we think of empathy as attention to communication and information, not as displays of emotional congruence.

Flexibility

Effective intercultural practitioners are flexible. Their thinking is flexible; they can conceive of different ways of perceiving, thinking, and feeling. They are open-minded. Without sacrificing their own values, they accept that other people may have different but deeply held values. Others may even have values that run counter to one's most deeply held values. Effective intercultural workers can adapt behavior to clients' cultures and co-cultures.

Being a People Person

As a child welfare worker, you are probably a people person. Cultural diversity is a testament to human adaptability and creativity. We hope becoming a cultural learner and skilled intercultural communicator will enhance your job effectiveness, open interesting worlds to you, and enable

Cultures, Co-cultures, and Genetics 151

you to sensitively handle genetic family history taking, genetic disorders, genetic services, and noncompliance with medical recommendation when assisting individuals and families of diverse cultural and co-cultural backgrounds.

Exercise 7. Genetics and Cultural Change

1. If you were born in the United States or immigrated as a child:
   - If you are 35 years old or older, what major changes have occured in your lifetime regarding in the health of infants, children, and adolescents?
   - What major changes regarding genetic disorders have occurred in your lifetime?
   - How has medical care changed for infants, children, and adolescents with genetic disorders?
   - What have been the major changes in health care financing? In attitudes toward genetic disorders and toward genetically affected people?
   - What are the major changes in law and policy concerning infants, children, and adolescents with genetic disorders? In what ways are the changes you have witnessed for the better? For the worse? What do you think has contributed to the changes that have occurred?

2. If you are 34 or younger, interview someone who is at least 20 years older than you (preferably older than that). Ask the questions above.

3. If you immigrated to the United States after you were 12:
   - What are the major differences in the health of infants, children, and adolescents between your country of origin and the United States?
   - How do members of your culture view genetic disorders?
   - How does the care of infants, children, and adolescents with genetic disorders in your country compare with the care given

in the United States? How does health care financing compare? The services available?
- How do the attitudes of your original culture toward genetic disorders and toward genetically affected people compare with U.S. American attitudes?
- Regarding children with genetic disorders, in what ways do you think your culture is superior? In what ways do you think U.S. American culture is superior?
- How has immigrating to the United States changed your attitudes toward genetic disorders, genetically affected people, and beliefs about the kind of care they should receive?

Exercise 8. Communication Behaviors

1. When you are standing and talking with a person, step closer. If the person backs away, step closer again. How do you feel while you are standing closer? What did the other person do? Later, do the same thing, only step away from the other person. How does greater distance make you feel? Ask the other person how she or he reacted to the changes in the interpersonal distance.

2. Try to describe a spiral staircase without using your hands.

3. While having a friendly conversation with a person, try not to smile. What is it like for you to not smile? How did the other person react? When the conversation in over, ask the other person what he or she thought was going on. How did your not smiling make that person feel?

4. During a conversation, talk more quietly than you normally do. What is it like for you to talk more quietly? How does the other person react? Then talk more loudly than usual. What is it like for you to talk more loudly? How did the other person react? How did the soft voice make him or her feel? The louder voice?

5. When talking with another person, delay your responses. Allow silences to develop. What is it like for you to experience silence? What does the other person do with the silences? How did the silences make her or him feel?

6. When talking with a friend, try not to use the words *I, me, my, mine,* or *myself* for five minutes. Were you able to do it? What was it like for you to avoid using words referring to yourself? How do you think people in familial-self cultures might view European Americans' frequent use of words referring to their individual selves?

Exercise 9. Your Intercultural Biography

1. Your ethnic identity: _____

2. Using the chart below, enter a plus (+) sign for each setting in which you have had a positive experience with a person from the co-cultures listed below. Use a minus sign (-) for settings in which you have had a negative experience. Enter both a plus and a minus sign (+/-) for settings in which you have had a mixed experience. In the blank squares, enter unlisted cultures or co-cultures with which you have had experiences.

	African American	Asian American	European American	Latino	Native American		
Family/Preschool							
K-6							
Middle School							
High School							
College/Grad School							
Military							
Work							
Personal Relationships							
Neighborhood							
Travel							
Born/Live Outside U.S.							

3. Looking at the chart, how much intercultural contact have you had? Where are the biggest gaps in your intercultural experiences?
4. Have your intercultural experiences been primarily positive or negative? How have these experiences influenced your perceptions and attitudes?

Exercise 10. Some Genetics and Culture Self-Awareness Questions

1. What is your co-cultural or co-cultural background?

2. What are your views on using prenatal diagnosis to determine if a fetus has a genetic disorder? What are the reasons for your views? Do other members of your culture or co-culture share your views? If not, why not? Might people from other cultures or co-cultures disagree with your views? How might their underlying values or world views differ from yours?

3. What are your views on termination of pregnancy for genetic reason? What are the reasons for your views? Do other members of your culture or co-culture share your views? If not, why not? Might people from other cultures or co-cultures disagree with your views? How might your values or world view differ from theirs?

4. What are your views on using heroic measures to keep alive babies who have serious birth defects? What are the reasons for your views? Do other members of your culture or co-culture share your views? If not, why not? Might people from other cultures or co-cultures disagree with your views? How might your values or world view differ from theirs?

5. If you had or have a child with a major disability, who would care for the child? Who would be or is involved in major decisions concerning the child? Would or do you make every effort to maximize the child's potential? Do other members of your culture or co-culture share your views? If not, why not? Might people from other cultures or co-cultures disagree with your views? How might your values or world view differ from theirs?

6. What are your views on the practice, in some countries, of allowing infants with birth defects to die? Do other members of your culture or co-culture share your views? If not, why not? How might your values or world view differ from those of people living in countries that allow or even encourage this practice?

7. What are your views on the Human Genome Project's goal of identifying every human gene? What do you think about manipulating human genes to prevent or cure genetic disorders? Do other members of your culture or co-culture share your views? If not, why not? Might people from other cultures or co-cultures disagree with you? How might your values or world view differ from theirs?

8. What are your views on using knowledge of genes to select healthy embryos for implantation into the uteri of women using infertility treatment? What about gender selection? Do other members of your culture or co-culture share your views? If not, why not? Might people from other cultures or co-cultures disagree with your views? In what ways might their underlying values or world view differ from yours?

9. The third step in self-knowledge is discovering the image we present to the rest of the world. How do others see you? A good starting point is your style of communication. Below are some questions to ask yourself. They are adapted from Samovar, Porter, and Stefani [1998].
    - Am I usually at ease or tense?
    - Do I dominate conversations, or am I relatively passive?
    - Do I often change the subject without taking the other person into consideration?
    - Do I smile often or seldom?
    - Do I interrupt repeatedly?
    - Do I speak softly or loudly?
    - Am I a good listener?
    - Do I show emotions and feelings, or am I reserved?
    - Do I often touch other people? How do I react when people touch me?

    Making an audiotape or videotape of a conversation is a wonderful way to learn about your communication style.

Exercise 11. Interview Mindfulness Questions

1. Does my culture or co-culture differ from my client's?
2. How am I reacting to my client's verbal and nonverbal communication behaviors? Am I uncomfortable, confused, or annoyed?
3. How am I interpreting my client's verbal and nonverbal communication behaviors?
4. What are some other possible interpretations? Are my client and I located at different points along the low context/high context communication continuum?
5. How might my client be reacting to and interpreting my verbal and nonverbal communication behaviors?
6. Do I need to modify any of my verbal or nonverbal communication behaviors? Which ones? In what way?

Appendix A
Organizations

This list is not all inclusive, nor do the authors endorse any particular organization or parent support group. More information can be found by conducting an Internet search or by contacting the Alliance of Genetic Support Groups, the National Organization for Rare Disorders, or the National Society of Genetic Counselors.

Attention-Deficit/Hyperactivity Disorder

Attention Deficit Disorder Association
P.O. Box 1303
Chicago, IL 60065-1303
E-mail: mail@add.org
www.add.org
(Note: When this book went to press, ADDA was in the process of moving its headquarters from Mentor, Ohio, to Chicago. Telephone numbers were not available.)

Children and Adults with Attention Deficit Disorder
8181 Professional Place, Suite 201
Landover, MD 20785
800/233-4050, 301/306-7070
Fax: 301/306-7090
E-mail: national@chadd.org
www.chadd.org

Autism

Autism Society of America
7910 Woodmont Avenue, Suite 300
Bethesda, MD 20814-3015
800/328-8467, 301/657-0881
Fax: 301/657-0869
E-mail: asa@smart.net
www.autism-society.org

Cerebral Palsy

Easter Seals
230 West Monroe Street, Suite 1800
Chicago, IL 60606-4802
800/221-6827, 312/726-6200
Fax: 312/726-1494; TTY: 312/726-4258
E-mail: info@easter-seals.org
www.easter-seals.org

United Cerebral Palsy
1660 L Street NW, Suite 700
Washington, DC 20036
800/872-5827, 202/776-0406
Fax: 202/776-0414; TTY: 202/973-7197
E-mail: ucpanatl@ucpa.org
www.ucpa.org

Child Health (General)

Association for the Care of Children's Health
P.O. Box 25707
Alexandria, VA 22313
800/808-2224
www.acch.org
(Note: ACCH was in the process of moving its headquarters when this book went to press.)

Deafness and Hearing Loss

Alexander Graham Bell Association for the Deaf, Inc.
3417 Volta Place, NW
Washington, DC 20007-2778
202/337-5220 (Voice/TTY)
Fax: 202/337-8314
E-mail: agbell2@aol.com
www.agbell.org

American Society for Deaf Children
1820 Tribute Road, Suite A
Sacramento, CA 95815
800/942-2732
916/641-6084 (Voice/TTY)
Fax: 916/641-6085
E-mail: asdc1@aol.com
http://deafchildren.org

Disabilities

Council for Exceptional Children
1920 Association Drive
Reston, VA 20191-1589
800/232-7733, 703/620-3660
Fax: 703/264-9494; TTY: 703/264-9446
E-mail: service@cec.sped.org
www.cec.sped.org

National Parent Network on Disabilities
1130 17th Street NW, Suite 400
Washington, DC 20036
202/463-2299 (Voice/TTY)
Fax: 202/463-9403
E-mail: npnd@cs.net
www.npnd.org

Down Syndrome

National Down Syndrome Congress
7000 Peachtree-Dunwoody Road NE
Lake Ridge 400 Office Park
Bldg. 5, Suite 100
Atlanta, GA 30328
800/232-6372, 770/604-9500
E-mail: ndsccenter@aol.com
www.carol.net/ndsc

National Down Syndrome Society
666 Broadway, 8th floor
New York, NY 10012-2317
800/221-4602, 212/460-9330
Fax: 212/979-2873
E-mail: info@ndss.org
www.ndss.org

Epilepsy

Epilepsy Foundation
4351 Garden City Drive
Landover, MD 20785
800/332-1000, 301/459-3700
Fax: 301/577-4941
E-mail: info@efa.org
www.efa.org

Genetic Disorders

March of Dimes
1275 Mamaroneck Avenue
White Plains, NY 10605
800/663-4637, 914/428-7100, 914/997-4764
Fax: 914/997-4410
E-mail: resourcecenter@modimes.org
www.modimes.org

National Organization for Rare Disorders
P.O. Box 8923
New Fairfield, CT 06812-8923
800/999-6673, 203/746-6518
Fax: 203/746-6481
E-mail: orphan@rarediseases.org
www.rarediseases.org

Genetic Support/Information Groups

Alliance of Genetic Support Groups
4301 Connecticut Avenue NW, Suite 404
Washington, DC 20008-2304
800/336-4363, 202/966-5557
Fax: 202/966-8553
E-mail: info@geneticalliance.org
www.geneticalliance.org

National Society of Genetic Counselors
233 Canterbury Drive
Wallingford, PA 19086-6617
610/872-7608
E-mail: nsgc@aol.com
www.nsgc.org
www.pitt.edu/~edugene/resource (Genetic Resource Center)

Learning Disabilities

Division for Learning Disabilities
Council for Exceptional Children
1920 Association Drive
Reston, VA 20191-1589
800/232-7733, 703/620-3660
Fax: 703/264-9494; TTY: 703/264-9446
E-mail: service@cec.sped.org
www.cec.sped.org

Appendix A

International Dyslexia Association (Formerly Orton Dyslexia Society)
Chester Building, Suite 382
8600 LaSalle Road
Baltimore, MD 21286-2044
800/222-3123, 410/296-0232
Fax: 410/321-5069
E-mail: info@interdys.org
http://www.interdys.org

Learning Disabilities Association of America
4156 Library Road
Pittsburgh, PA 15234-1349
412/341-1515
Fax: 412/341-0224
E-mail: ldanatl@usaor.net
www.ldanatl.org

Mental Health

American Academy of Child and Adolescent Psychiatry
Public Information Office
3615 Wisconsin Avenue NW
Washington, DC 20016-3007
800/333-7636, 202/966-7300
Fax: 202/966-2891
E-mail: communications@aacap.org
www.aacap.org

National Alliance for the Mentally Ill
200 North Glebe Road, Suite 1015
Arlington, VA 22203-3754
800/95-6264, 703/524-7600
Fax: 703/524-9094; TTY: 703/516-7227
E-mail: membership@nami.org
www.nami.org

National Mental Health Association
1021 Prince Street
Alexandria, VA 22314-2971
800/969-6642, 703/684-7722
Fax: 703/684-5968; TTY: 800/433-5959
E-mail: info@nmha.org
www.nmha.org

Mental Retardation

American Association on Mental Retardation
444 North Capitol Street NW, Suite 846
Washington, DC 20001-1512
800/424-3688, 202/387-1968
Fax: 202/387-2193
E-mail: anam@aamr.org
www.aamr.org

The ARC
500 East Border Street, Suite 300
Arlington, TX 76010
800/433-5255, 817/261-6003
Fax: 817/277-3491; TTY: 817/277-0553
E-mail: thearc@matronet.com
http://thearc.org

Multiple Disabilities

TASH-Disability Advocacy World Wide
29 West Susquehanna Avenue, Suite 210
Baltimore, MD 21204
410/828-8274
Fax: 410/828-6706; TTY 410/828-1306
E-mail: info@tash.org
www.tash.org

Speech and Language Disorders

Alliance for Technology Access
2175 East Francisco Boulevard, Suite L
San Rafael, CA 94901
800/455-7970, 415/455-4575
Fax: 415/455-0654; TTY: 415/455-0491
E-mail: atainfo@ataccess.org
www.ataccess.org

American Cleft Palate-Craniofacial Association, Cleft Palate Foundation
104 South Estes Drive, Suite 204
Chapel Hill, NC 27514
800/242-5338, 919/933-9044
Fax: 919/933-9604
E-mail: cleft@aol.com
www.cleft.com

Spina Bifida

Spina Bifida Association of America
4590 MacArthur Boulevard NW, Suite 250
Washington, DC 20007-4226
800/621-3141, 202/944-3285
Fax: 202/944-3295
E-mail: sbaa@sbaa.org
www.sbaa.org

Visual Impairments

American Foundation for the Blind
11 Penn Plaza, Suite 300
New York, NY 10001
800/232-5463, 212/502-7600
Fax: 212/502-7774
E-mail: afbinfo@afb.net
www.afb.org

Blind Children's Center
4120 Marathon Street
Los Angeles, CA 90029-3584
800/222-3566, 323/664-2153
Fax: 323/665-3828
E-mail: info@blindchildrenscenter.org
www.blindchildrenscenter.org

Division for the Visually Handicapped
Council for Exceptional Children
1920 Association Drive
Reston, VA 20191-1589
800/232-7733, 703/620-3660
Fax: 703/264-9494; TTY: 703/264-9446
E-mail: service@cec.sped.org
www.cec.sped.org

National Federation of the Blind
1800 Johnson Street
Baltimore, MD 21230
410/659-9314
Fax: 410/685-5653
E-mail: nfb@inmdigex.net
www.nfb.org

Appendix B
Genetic Family History, Long Form

Family History Form Instructions*

The purpose of the Family History Form is to assist the practitioner to make a decision as to whether a more detailed genetic evaluation is required and to provide information to physicians; biological, foster, and adoptive parents; and adult adoptees so that, in the future, appropriate health care can be obtained.

1. **Check if Yes.** Put a check mark beside each condition that any relative of the child (family member or other blood relative) has had.
2. **Relationship to Child.** Enter the relationship to the child of the person who has the condition. For example, maternal grandmother, paternal aunt, or half-sister. If the relative is not a member of the nuclear family, be sure to identify which side of the family the relative is on (maternal or paternal). Do not enter the person's name.
3. **Age at Onset.** Enter the age at which the condition first appeared. If the exact age is unknown, enter the best information that the informant can give you, for example, "in her teens," or "when he was old." Age at onset is a key factor in evaluation of genetic disorders. For example, cataracts before age 50 are more likely to be associated with a specific genetic disorder than cataracts at age 70. This type of information is helpful to adopted people as they get older.

---

* Protocol prepared by Karen Hoffman, M.D., Johns Hopkins Hospital, Baltimore, Maryland.

4. **Comments and Name of Disorder (if known).** If at all possible, try to obtain a specific name for the disorder, even if it is not the usual medical term. It can be helpful even if it is only a colloquial term such as "low sugar" or "low blood." If a child or a relative has some type of "syndrome," try to note the features, such as "ears are unusually wide apart" or "born with cataracts."

When to Refer to a Genetics Center

- **If specific disorders have been circled** in the family history or in the ethnic origins screen.
- **If the child or a relative has a birth defect.**
- **If the age of onset of a particular condition in a family is in childhood or adolescence**; for example, deafness or blindness.

When to Call a Genetics Center and Discuss with a Genetic Counselor

- **If more than one family member** (which may or may not include the child) has any of the same problems; for example, heart problems, breast cancer, or mental illness. The counselor can advise you how to proceed.
- **If a clear pattern can be seen in the family history**; for example, if only males are affected by deafness or if siblings have webbed fingers or toes.

Ethnic Origins Screen

Some conditions are more common in certain ethnic groups than in the population as a whole. Sometimes, a person may be healthy but carry a gene for an inherited disorder that could occur in his or her children if the other parent also happens to be a carrier. Carrier screening is available for certain conditions so individuals can learn if they are carriers for these disorders.

Following is a list of selected disorders commonly found in people of certain ethnic origins. This list does not include all disorders in certain ethnic groups, just the more common ones. Circle the child's ethnic

Appendix B

origins. Remember that the child may have more than one ethnic origin. In that case, circle all that apply. Ask whether the listed disease(s) has/have occurred in the family.

- Africa
  - sickle cell disease
  - Thalassemia (try also Cooley's anemia or low blood count, or "needed many transfusions or iron for many years")
- Mediterranean (Greece, Italy, France, Spain, Yugoslavia, Turkey)
  - sickle cell disease
  - Thalassemia
- Caribbean
  - sickle cell disease
  - Thalassemia
- India
  - sickle cell disease
  - Thalassemia
- Middle East
  - sickle cell disease
  - Thalassemia
- Asia: China, Japan, Southeast Asia
-   Thalassemia
- Ashkenazi Jewish
  - Tay-Sachs disease
  - Gaucher disease (adult form)
- Europe and United Kingdom
  - Phenylketonuria (PKU)
  - cystic fibrosis
- French-Canadian
  - Tay-Sachs disease
- Native American
  - diabetes (try also sugar diabetes, high blood sugar)

FAMILY HISTORY FORM

Name of Child _____

Disorder	Check if Yes	Relationship to Child	Age of Onset	Comments & Name of Disorder (if known)
Birth defects (i.e., was born with) Spina bifida (open spine defect)				
Misshapen skull				
Kidney/bladder				
Heart				
Fingers or toes; e.g., webbing, extra, missing				
Cleft palate				
Cleft lip				
Ears—tags (pieces of skin) or pits next to ear				
Other (specify)				
Syndromes Down syndrome				
Other (individuals whose features are dissilimar from rest of family)				

FAMILY HISTORY FORM *continued*

Name of Child _____

Disorder	Check if Yes	Relationship to Child	Age of Onset	Comments & Name of Disorder (if known)
Eyes				
Blindness				
Cataracts				
Night blindness				
Extremely far- or nearsighted; serious visual problems				
Glaucoma				
Retinal detachment				
Other				
Ears				
Deafness, hearing loss				
Other				
Hair, skin, teeth				
Numerous lumps, bumps				
Premature balding or greying				
White patch of hair				
Teeth (extra, missing, misshapen)				

FAMILY HISTORY FORM *continued*

Name of Child _____

Disorder	Check if Yes	Relationship to Child	Age of Onset	Comments & Name of Disorder (if known)
Hair, skin, teeth (continued) Tooth loss in early adulthood				
Birth marks (pink, brown, white)				
Other				
Nervous system Learning disability				
Mental retardation				
Seizures (convulsions, epilepsy)				
Shaking/twitching				
Episodes of coma				
Stroke				
Alcoholism				
Manic depression, depression				
Schizophrenia, mental illness				
Speech difficulty				

FAMILY HISTORY FORM *continued*

Name of Child _____

Disorder	Check if Yes	Relationship to Child	Age of Onset	Comments & Name of Disorder (if known)
Nervous system (continued) Alzheimer's, presenile dementia				
Other				
Muscle, bone Loss of strength or control of muscles				
Brittle bone, history of broken bones				
Growth (too short or tall compared with rest of family)				
Loose joints, double jointed				
Other				
Allergies Hayfever				
Asthma				
Eczema				
Allergy to medication				
Died while under anesthesia				
Other				

FAMILY HISTORY FORM *continued*

Name of Child _____

Disorder	Check if Yes	Relationship to Child	Age of Onset	Comments & Name of Disorder (if known)
Lungs				
Cystic fibrosis				
Other				
Digestion				
Ulcers				
Colitis				
High cholesterol				
Restricted or special diet				
Other				
Endocrine				
Sugar diabetes				
Thyroid problems				
Other				
Blood				
Bleeding without injury, or bleeding more than expected after injury or hemophilia				
Anemia requiring treatment such, as iron or frequent transfusion				
Other				

FAMILY HISTORY FORM *continued*

Name of Child _____

Disorder	Check if Yes	Relationship to Child	Age of Onset	Comments & Name of Disorder (if known)
Cardiovascular High blood presssure				
Heart attack or serious heart problem before age 50				
Other				
Cancer Breast cancer				
Colon cancer				
Other growth or tumor				
Kidneys Polycystic kidneys				
Kidney stones				
Kidney failure, dialysis				
Other				

Was a geneticist or genetic counselor consulted regarding this family?   ☐ NO   ☐ YES
If YES, summarize recommendations.

Appendix C
Recommendations for Obtaining, Storing, and Transmitting Genetic Information

The recommendations in this appendix have been adapted from those developed at the workshop, "Genetics and Adoption: Every Child Potentially a Special Needs Child," held May 3–5, 1990, in Washington, D.C.

Recommendations for Gathering Genetic Information

Basic Principle

Everyone has the right to know his or her genetic history.

Issue 1. What information needs to be gathered?

All health and genetic information relative to the needs of the adoptee, both as a child and as an adult, should be gathered.

Issue 2. When should information be gathered?

Information should be gathered at the earliest point of contact and should continue on an ongoing basis, whenever possible.

Issue 3. Who should gather the information?

Some members of the task group felt social workers should gather the information. Others felt that the geneticist should gather the information because there are times when the social worker has an adversarial relationship with the birth family. The recommendation was that social workers should gather the primary information but should consult and coordinate with geneticists.

Issue 4. How should the information be gathered?

One uniform instrument should be developed and used as widely as possible. A two-step approach is needed. Several groups, subcommittees, and state child welfare programs are developing instruments; these should be collected and disseminated for use as soon as possible.

The second step is to implement a follow-up project to develop and disseminate one uniform instrument for use in the field.

Issue 5. What should be done with the initial information once it has been obtained?

The social worker should review the information and confer with a genetics professional regarding any question that may bear upon placement and should also appropriately refer for guidance for genetic assessment and treatment.

Information on resources should be available. Networks among social workers, genetics professionals, and parent support groups should be cultivated to facilitate consultation and referral.

Issue 6. Hard data about the incidence of genetic disorders in adoptees, their access to needed genetic services, and the availability of biological family genetic histories are needed.

We must move beyond anecdotal data to more effectively influence federal, state, and local governing bodies. Information regarding Issue 6 should be obtained from several populations: genetic service providers; health care professionals, including nurses and pediatricians; adoptive parents; child welfare professionals; and national professional organizations.

Issue 7. How can funds be obtained for service provision, research, education, and training?

An effort should be made to identify existing funding resources, such as Medicaid, and work to broaden coverage to include genetic services and also to lobby for appropriations to be made in federal discretionary grant programs and in state health programs. Foundations and other funding sources that might be interested in specific projects in genetics and adoption should be identified.

Issue 8. How should social workers be educated and trained in genetics?

Genetic content should be included in all levels of social work education—undergraduate, graduate, and postgraduate. Existing curriculum content should be reviewed and efforts undertaken to mandate the integration of genetic content into social work curricula. Genetic content should be included in training and continuing education programs. Field placements in genetic counseling and genetic disorder clinics should be developed. Efforts should be made to conduct workshops at regional and national professional conferences.

Issue 9. On the whole, there is little communication about genetics and adoption issues and practices between child welfare professionals, geneticists, and the medical community.

Articles dealing with this content from an interdisciplinary perspective should be written for submission to social work, genetics, pediatric, and other journals.

Issue 10. What should be done when birth parents are not available to provide genetic information?

Use any other available resources, within legal and ethical constraints. These might include relatives, other available records, and routine pediatric screenings. In abandonment situations, information should be obtained through appropriate screening tests for children from groups known to be at high risk for specific disorders.

Recommendations for Storing, Updating, and Postadoption Accessing of Information

Basic Principle

Adoption is a lifelong process; umbilical cords are very long and very tough. Everyone has the right to genetic information that pertains to his or her health, medical care, and reproductive decision making and to the health, medical care, and reproductive decision making of her or his offspring.

Issue 1. Where should information be stored?
- Mutual-consent adoption registries should be established in states that do not have them.
- Even in states with mutual-consent adoption registries, agencies should maintain full records, including genetic and medical histories.
- The inclusion in court records of information about where the information is stored should be encouraged. Requiring information be stored by the court should be considered.
- Policies pertaining to the storage of medical and genetic information in private adoptions need to be formulated.

Issue 2. What information should be stored?
- Stored records should include medical and genetic information. Because hospitals purge their records periodically, the medical and genetic records should be as comprehensive as possible.
- Medical and genetic records should be stored in the placement agency if state law does not provide for storage in court records or in a birth registry.
- An effort should be made to develop a uniform protocol for recording and storing genetic information.

Issue 3. How should information be updated?
- Birth parents, adoptive parents, and adopted individuals should be encouraged to inform the registry or agency of any genetic diagnoses or other genetic information that may have significance for the health of birth family members or their reproductive decision making.
- Geneticists who diagnose a genetic condition in an adopted person or a person in which a member of the birth family was adopted away should encourage the individual or family to inform the storage resource (placement agency, court, or adoption registry).

Issue 4. Who should have access to the genetic information?
- Access belongs to the adult adopted person, adoptive parents of the minor child, birth parents, and the progeny of both the adopted individual and the birth parents.
- No identifying information should be released without consent of the individuals concerned.
- Access must include the individual's right not to know.
- When genetic or medical information is provided, the social worker or other provider should be aware that the information may be outdated and that increased capabilities may mean that better information can be obtained, and the social worker should so inform the client.
- When the record indicates that the person may be at genetic risk, the person should be informed that genetic assessment and counseling are available.

Issue 5. Can confidentiality be guaranteed?
- Complex legal and ethical issues of confidentiality exist, as are questions of liability because of failure to disclose.
- Biological parents should be informed that nonidentifying family medical and genetic information will be provided to the adoptive parents and to the adopted individual.
- No identifying information should be provided without the explicit consent of the involved person.
- When consent for release of information is refused, the obligation to disclose because of threat to the health or lives of other people may override the guarantee of confidentiality.
- Guidelines should be developed for situations in which the obligation to disclose overrides guarantees of confidentiality.

Formulated by the Task Group on Storing, Updating, and Accessing Genetic Information. Note: The task group did not address the question of banking samples of parental DNA, which could be examined by methods that may be developed in the future.

Recommendations for Transmitting Genetic Information

Basic Principle

Adoptive parents and adopted individuals must comprehend any genetic information presented to them and its psychosocial, health, and developmental ramifications for reproductive decision making.

Issue 1. Who should transmit genetic information, and when should it be transmitted?

- The process of transmitting genetic information takes place over time. Information should be given in graduated steps as appropriate for the stage in the adoption process, and by qualified members of the adoption team. Transmittal of information to adoptive parents should be regarded as a team effort involving the adoptive child worker; the adoptive home worker; health professionals such as geneticists, pediatricians, or genetic counselors; and possibly education professionals, psychotherapists, and foster parents.
- The transmittal of genetic information should not be the sole responsibility of the social worker. Transmittal is a team effort but the social worker should take the lead and act as team coordinator.
- At the first presentation of a child to a prospective adoptive family, the adoptive home caseworker should give a profile of the child without detailed genetic information, unless the information is significant to the child's placement.
- If the family is interested, a team presentation should follow, with the adoptive child worker taking the lead, but including the adoptive home worker and the appropriate health professional(s).
- If the child is placed, and depending on the child's developmental age at the time of placement, a second meeting should occur between the child's worker, health professional, adoptive parents, and other members of the team who have significant information.

Issue 2. What information should be transmitted to the adoptive parents?
- All nonidentifying information known at the time of referral or placement (medical, genetic, educational, and case records) should be presented initially during an in-person meeting. The information should be interpreted and its implications discussed.
- There should be a balance between presentation of genetic risks and problems. Information on the child's current adaptive functioning and potential—both "negative" and "positive" information—should be given.

Issue 3. How should information be presented?
- This complex information should be presented in terms that can be understood by people without backgrounds in genetics, avoiding use of unnecessary technical language, and providing clear definitions of any technical terminology used.
- Adoptive parents should be questioned to determine if they understand the information.
- The information should be presented in several ways to encourage understanding and retention; information given verbally should also be put in writing.
- All information should be organized into a summary profile that presents the child as a whole person and includes medical and genetic information.
- Information should be presented within a life-span framework and should highlight future implications, especially for reproductive decision making and developmental transitions.
- If the parent(s) agree, the presentation should be tape recorded and given to the parents for review.

Issue 4. How should the genetic information be given to the child?
- It is the responsibility of the adoptive family to decide what and when to share, just as in the case with birth children.
- Every effort should be made to ensure that the adoptive parents have the information needed to answer the child's questions.

- This information should be given by the adoptive parents in response to a child's queries and in an age-appropriate manner.

Issue 5. What about the older adolescent or adult adoptee?
- Older adolescents or adult adoptees should be informed of the option of meeting with a genetic counselor to answer any questions they might have;
- Genetic information should be presented in an in-person interview, not just through written records.

Issue 6. What about liability?
- Genetic information is complex; many people have difficulty grasping it. Agencies and workers need to protect themselves against allegations of providing inadequate or misleading information.
- Genetic information should be presented in a process of increasing technicality, with the genetics professional sharing in presentation and interpretation.
- Information should be presented without absolutes but in terms of probabilities.
- Parents should be told that the information may become outdated due to the changing nature of genetic and medical capabilities.
- "Red flag" indicators of possible problems should be highlighted; recommendations about responses to such indicators should be provided.
- Provide information on support groups, benefits, social resources, and possible future needs.

Issue 7. What about the birth parents' right to confidentiality?
- The right to confidentiality of the birth parent versus the well-being of the adopted child should be considered.
- Identifying information should be deleted from all preadoption medical, education, and case records.
- The birth family should be told that nonidentifying medical and genetic information will be shared with the adoptive family.

- The adoptive family should be alerted to the implications of having extensive information about the child and the birth family—with whom the information should be shared; who will have access to the information; when and how to share the information with the child; and the chances of the child learning the information from other people, including professionals, before the parents give it to the child.
- Legislation should be enacted to allow the option of mutual consent, open information, and access to nonidentifying information

Issue 8. What should be done if a genetic diagnosis is obtained after the adoption is final?

- Mechanisms should be established to enable transmission of genetic information, obtained after the adoption is final, to the adopted individual, the adoptive family, or the birth family;
- Guidelines should be developed for transmitting genetic information when patients or clients do not give consent to contacting biological relatives for whom the information may be significant.

Issue 9. What are the education and training needs?

- Any social worker who is involved in transmitting genetic information should be trained in basic genetic concepts, genetic services and capabilities, and the psychosocial aspects of relatively common conditions;
- All medical and genetic professionals involved in transmitting information to adopted individuals and adoptive parents should be trained in child welfare policies; the adoption process; information-related issues, including possible liability and wrongful adoption suits; and presentation skills.
- Potential adoptive families should be educated about inheritance and psychosocial aspects of genetic disorders before they are presented with a child.

Issue 10. Is legislative change needed?

- Consideration should be given to enacting state and federal legislation to mandate obtaining genetic family histories and any needed genetic evaluations for all types of adoptions.

Formulated by the Task Group on Issues of Gathering Genetic Information

Appendix D
Federal Information Centers and Clearinghouses

Alcohol, Drugs, & Substance Abuse

National Clearinghouse for Alcohol and Drug Information
P.O. Box 2345
Rockville, MD 20847-2345
800/729-6686
Fax: 301/468-6433; TTY: 800/487-4889
E-mail: info@prevline.health.org
www.health.org

Allergy & Infectious Disease

National Institute of Allergy and Infectious Diseases (NIAID)
31 Center Drive, MSC 2520
Bethesda, MD 20892-2520
301/496-5717
Fax: 301/402-0120
www.niaid.nih.gov

Arthritis

National Arthritis and Musculoskeletal and Skin Diseases Information Clearinghouse
1 AMS Circle
Bethesda, MD 20892-3675
301/495-4484
Fax: 301/718-6366; TTY: 301/565-2966
www.nih.gov/niams/healthinfo/info.htm

Blindness

National Library Service for the Blind and Physically Handicapped
Library of Congress
1291 Taylor Street NW
Washington, DC 20542
202/707-5100
Fax: 202/707-0712
E-mail: nls@loc.gov
www.loc.gov/nls

Children and Youth with Disabilities

National Information Center for Children and Youth with Disabilities
P.O. Box 1492
Washington, DC 20013-1492
800/695-0285, 202/884-8200
Fax: 202/884-8441
E-mail: nichcy@aed.org
www.nichcy.org

Deafness

National Information Center on Deafness
Gallaudet University
800 Florida Avenue NE
Washington, DC 20002
202/651-5051
Fax: 202/651-5054; TTY: 202/651-5052
E-mail: pcnmp.product@gallaudet.edu
www.gallaudet.edu/~nicd

National Institute on Deafness and Other Communication Disorders Clearinghouse
National Institutes of Health
31 Center Drive, MSC 2320
Bethesda, MD 20892-2320
301/496-7243
Fax: 301/402-0018; TTY: 301/402-0252
www.nih.gov/nidcd

Diabetes

National Diabetes Information Clearinghouse
1 Information Way
Bethesda, MD 20892-3560
301/654-3327
Fax: 301/907-8906
E-mail: ndic@info.niddk.nih.gov
www.niddk.nih.gov/health/diabetes/ndic.htm

Disabilities

Clearinghouse on Disability Information
U.S. Department of Education
Office of Special Education and Rehabilitative Services
Switzer Building, Room 3132
330 C Street SW
Washington, DC 20202-2524
202/205-8241
Fax: 202/401-2608
www.ed.gov/offices/OSERS

Heart, Lung, and Blood

National Heart, Lung, and Blood Institute Information Center
P.O. Box 30105
Bethesda, MD 20824-0105
301/592-8573
Fax: 301/592-8563
E-mail: NHLBIinfo@rover.nhlbi.nih.gov
www.nhlbi.nih.gov

Kidney and Urological Diseases

National Kidney and Urologic Diseases Information Clearinghouse
3 Information Way
Bethesda, MD 20892-3560
301/654-4415
Fax: 301/907-8906
www.niddk.nih.gov/health/kidney/nkudic.htm

Maternal and Child Health

National Center for Education in Maternal and Child Health
2000 15th Street North, Suite 701
Arlington, VA 22201-2617
703/524-7802
Fax: 703/524-9335
E-mail: info@ncemch.org
www.ncemch.org

National Maternal and Child Health Clearinghouse
2070 Chain Bridge Road, Suite 450
Vienna, VA 22182-2536
888/434-4624, 703/356-1964
Fax: 703/821-2098
E-mail: nmchc@cirsol.com
www.nmchc.org

Mental Health

National Institute of Mental Health
6001 Executive Blvd., Room 8184, MSC 9663
Bethesda, MD 20892-9663
301/443-4513
Fax: 301/443-4279
E-mail:nimhinfo@nih.gov
www.nimh.nih.gov

Center for Mental Health Services Knowledge Exchange Network
P.O. Box 42490
Washington, DC 20015
800/789-2647
Fax: 301/984-8796; TTY: 301/443-9006
E-mail: ken@mentalhealth.org
www.mentalhealth.org

Military Family Resource Center
4040 North Fairfax Drive
Arlington, VA 22203-1635
703/696-9053
Fax: 703/696-9062
E-mail: mfrc@hq.odedodea.edu
www.mfrc.calib.com

Appendix E
Recommended Readings

General

- Batshaw, M.L. (Ed.). (1997). *Children with disabilities* (4th ed.). Baltimore: Paul H. Brookes Publishing Company.

This book is intended for professionals involved with children who have disabilities. Part I discusses heredity, threats to healthy prenatal development, low birthweight and small size for gestational-age infants, and the first few weeks of life. Part II discusses the impact of maternal substance abuse and of HIV/AIDS on the developing child and reviews normal development of critical systems and functions, such as language. Part III discusses major developmental disabilities and their care requirements. The final section discusses interventions. Helpful appendixes include brief descriptions of many syndromes; use, dosage, and common side effects of commonly medications; and resources for children with disabilities. This invaluable reference is recommended for child welfare department offices or libraries.

- Boston Children's Hospital. (1987). *The new child health encyclopedia: The complete guide for parents.* New York: Dell Publishing.

This parents guide briefly reviews normal child development, basic health care, accident prevention, choosing and using health care, first aid, and emergency care. The book describes various health conditions and their care. This is a clearly written, concise, helpful resource that child welfare workers can use to obtain a snapshot of specific health conditions and their care requirements.

- Children's Defense Fund. (1989). *94-142 and 504: Numbers that add up to educational rights for children with disabilities. A guide for parents and advocates.* Washington, DC: Author.

This 53-page brochure reviews the rights of children with disabilities, eligibility for free public school services, school districts' responsibilities, the evaluation and planning processes, and steps in the appeal process. It also contains lists of organizational resources and legal references.

- Green, M. (Ed.). (1994). *Bright futures: Guidelines for health supervision of infants, children, and adolescents.* Arlington, VA: National Center for Education in Maternal and Child Health.

Bright Futures is a national effort to enable those who care for children—parents as well as professionals—to be more effective in disease prevention and health promotion. For each life stage, this book reviews normal development, family preparation for health supervision, developmental strengths and issues, questions for the health care provider to ask during the health supervision visit, anticipatory guidance for the family, and what to look for in observing parent-child interaction. Clear, concise, simply written, this guide belongs on the desk of every child welfare worker.

- McCreight, B. (1997). *Recognizing and managing children with fetal alcohol syndrome/fetal alcohol effects: A guidebook.* Washington, DC: Child Welfare League of America.

This important guide offers practical advice and solid information for dealing with the lifelong effects of fetal alcohol syndrome and fetal alcohol effects on behavior and learning. It covers the historical, medical, and social aspects of FAS/FAE and details the common behavioral characteristics associated with the condition. Taking a developmental approach, the guide offers specific behavioral management techniques to be used with children with FAS/FAE from infancy through late adolescence. The author's own case studies are used to clarify psychological concepts and personalize FAS/FAE for the novice.

- Pueschel, S.M.; Scola, K.P.; Weidenman, L.E.; & Berneir, J.C. (1995). *The special child: a source book for parents of children with developmental* disabilities (2nd ed.). Baltimore: Paul H. Brookes Publishing Company.

This home reference includes specific information on the detection, prognosis, and treatment of various conditions. It also provides information on education, intervention, advocacy, financial planning, and medical and technological advances that may affect the lives of children with special health care needs.

- U.S. Department of Education. (1992). *Summary of existing legislation affecting people with disabilities* (Publication No. ED/OSERS 92-8). Washington, DC: U.S. Government Printing Office.

This comprehensive guide summarizes federal legislation in a variety of areas: education, employment, health, housing, income maintenance, nutrition, rights, social services, transportation, vocational rehabilitation, and miscellaneous topics. Because Congress has enacted changes in some laws, workers should contact the Clearinghouse on Disability Information (see Appendix D) to verify the law as it pertains to specific clients.

- Turnball, A.P., & Turnball, H.R., III. (1986). *Families, professionals, and exceptionality: A special partnership.* Columbus, OH: Merrill Publishing Company.

This clearly written book reviews the impact of chronic illness, disabilities, and handicapping conditions upon children and their families. It is primarily concerned with effective parent-professional collaboration and has two chapters on communication skills and strategies and how to present information to families. In the context of the education of the handicapped law, the book also offers hands-on discussions of the referral and evaluation process, due process and the law, and helping families cope. This book will assist the child welfare worker interested in accessing needed services and in helping parents and caretakers to cope.

- Turner, F.J. (Ed.). (1989). *Child psychopathology: A social work perspective.* New York: The Free Press.

Chapters written by social work experts discuss psychological disorders of children, including mental retardation, autism, affective disorders, schizophrenia, substance abuse, and suicide. The format for each chapter varies, but in general each describes the condition, reviews theories of causes, discusses the impact on the family, and summarizes appropriate social work interventions. Each chapter has an extensive bibliography. Although learning disabilities, ADHD, and attachment disorders are not covered, this reference is a good starting point for the worker who wants a quick orientation to children's psychological problems.

- Wallace, H.M.; Green, G.; Jaros, K.; Paine, L.L.; & Story, M. (Eds.). (1998). *Health and welfare for families in the 21st century*. Sudbury, MA: Jones and Bartlett Publishers.

This treasure trove of information is the starting point for any person interested in children's health and welfare. It is divided into six sections: Foundations, Social Welfare, Health Expenditures and Insurance, Health Issues and Policy Implications, Programs and Initiatives, and Summing Up. Chapters are written by nationally recognized experts who provide concise, informative summaries of given topics and discuss policy and program implications. Topics include health care issues pertaining to children in out-of-home care, child care, child abuse and neglect, homeless women and children, and children and managed care.

- Wallace, H.M.; Biehl, R.F.; MacQueen, J.C.; & Blackman, J.A. (1997). *Mosby's resource guide to children with disabilities and chronic illness*. St. Louis, MO: Mosby-Yearbook, Inc.

The first 40 pages of this book provide capsule summaries of programs, policies, and issues affecting children with special health care needs, such as legal rights of children with disabilities, case management, genetic services, and vocational training of students with disabilities. It also describes several serious conditions and their management and, in a separate section, describes the training and roles of various health care providers. This reference is highly recommended for child welfare workers who want quick, readable information about the types of services that children with disabilities and chronic illnesses need.

Genetics

- Barth, J.C. (1993). *"It runs in my family." Overcoming the legacy of family illness*. New York: Brunner/Mazel, Publishers.

This book is intended for members of the general public who are concerned about health conditions that "run in the family." In highly readable text, it provides an overview of inheritance, gives instructions for drawing a genogram, discusses common feelings and fears, and suggests ways to maximize one's health. Each chapter concludes with activities for obtaining family health information, identifying one's concerns, relieving stress, and healthy living. Appendixes include a form for assessing one's health, a list of information sources about familial disorders, and a checklist for professionals to assess their own functioning in five areas: medical care, stress management, work, family, and friends. Recommended for people interested in their own family health histories.

Child Welfare and Genetics

- Burns, J.K., & Reiser, C.A. (1992). Continuing education in genetics for adoption workers in Wisconsin. *Journal of Genetic Counseling, 1* (2), 187–209.

After Wisconsin enacted legislation requiring collection of medical-genetic histories at the time of termination of parental rights, statewide training in genetics was provided to adoption workers. Introductory content was offered at five sites. The program also offered two optional advanced training opportunities, which included observing at a genetics center. Comparisons of genetic family histories taken by trained and untrained workers suggested the training was effective.

- DeWoody, M. (1993). *Adoption and disclosure: A review of the law.* Washington, DC: Child Welfare League of America.

Quality adoption practice supports sharing of information so children with medical, psychological, and developmental problems are placed with families prepared to meet their needs. This report offers a needed overview of the legal developments around disclosure of health and background information in adoption. Part I reviews the major court decisions in this area and summarizes judicial trends. Part II reviews statutory law and charts the various ways in which states have defined the nature and scope of duty to disclose nonidentifying information.

- Freundlich, M., & Peterson, L. (1998). *Wrongful adoption: Law, policy, and practice.* Washington, DC: CWLA Press.

The past decade has seen an increase in cases where adoptive parents fail to receive accurate or complete information about a child's physical, emotional, or development problem, or about a child's birth family and history. In such cases, adoptive parents, confronted with extremely expensive medical care or mental health care, have sought assistance through the courts. This book examines the issue in four parts: the history of adoption practice in relation to disclosure of children's health and other background information, cases that have shaped the law of wrongful adoption, key policy and practice issues, and recommendations for quality practice.

- Kopels, S. (1995). Wrongful adoption: Litigation and liability. *Families in Society, 76,* (1), 20–29.

This article reviews the concept of liability as defined in wrongful adoption cases. The definition has expanded to include agencies' negligent conduct in failing to disclose information about children they place for adoption. To date, no court has found that agencies have a duty to discover background information about a child. With the increasing number of state statutes permitting disclosure, however, courts may come to view a disclosure status as creating the duty to discover. Courts have upheld wrongful adoption suits based on failure to disclose genetic information. Agencies and workers can take various actions in the areas of guidelines, policy development, and training to limit their liability.

- Rauch, J.B. (Ed.). (1991). *Genetics and adoption: Every child potentially a special needs child.* Proceedings of a workshop held May 3–5, 1990, in Washington, D.C. Sponsored by the School of Social Work, University of Maryland at Baltimore.

Includes the proceedings of a conference for genetics and child welfare professionals in the mid-Atlantic region, including papers on ethical issues, teaching models, and barriers to delivering genetic services to children in out-of-home care. The participants formulated recommendations for obtaining, storing, and transmitting genetic information during the adoption process. (See Appendix C.) Although out-of-print, photocopies are available at cost by contacting the Maryland School of Social Work.

- Rauch, J.B., & Plumridge, D. (1992). A project to strengthen linkages between genetic centers and child welfare services. *Journal of Genetic Counseling, 1* (2), 169–186.

This article describes a project linking genetic centers and child welfare services in the mid-Atlantic region. The model could be applied at the state and local levels.

Psychosocial Needs and Services

Many print resources are available that deal with the psychosocial aspects of chronic illnesses, disabilities, and handicapping conditions in general. Those listed here provide broad frameworks that can be applied across conditions. The Schild and Black book (page 199) discusses psychosocial issues characteristic of genetic disorders in general. The books should be in your local library or obtainable through interlibrary loans, local bookstores, or Internet booksellers.

Some psychosocial issues, such as genetic identity, pertain to all genetic disorders. Other issues are disorder-specific. The journal literature is voluminous but is largely disorder specific. Also available are books, often in paperback and directed at parents and the general public, that focus on relatively common conditions, such as sickle cell disease and ADHD. For reasons of space, disorder-specific resources are not listed here. If you are interested in psychosocial aspects of a specific condition, the National Center for Education in Maternal and Child Health (Appendix D, page 190) will conduct a free search of its holdings and send you copies of articles and book chapters. The National Maternal and Child Health Clearinghouse (Appendix D, page 190) can also send information about some conditions. National, state, and local organizations concerned with genetic disorders in general or specific conditions are also invaluable resources. (See Appendixes A and D and Quick Reference #6.)

- Bernhardt, B., & Rauch, J.B. (1993). Genetic family histories: An aid to social work assessment. *Families in Society,* 74 (4), 195–205.

   The authors discuss the rationale for obtaining genetic family histories during assessment and the harms that can result when family health information is not obtained. They also discuss approaches to obtaining and recording genetic family histories, present criteria for referral to genetic services, and recommend that agency administrators develop a genetic family history protocol and provide in-service training in genetics. A format for obtaining and recording genetic family histories is included. This article offers a more concise presentation of the information provided in this *Guide* and is suitable for use by agency staff who are unfamiliar with genetics, genetic services, and taking genetic family histories.

- Bishop, K.K. (1993). Psychosocial aspects of genetic disorders: Implications for practice. *Families in Society,* 74 (4), 207–212.

   The author reviews the research concerned with the psychosocial aspects of genetic disorders. Case examples illustrate the many services that social workers can provide to individuals and families affected by or at risk for genetic disorders. The article offers recommendations to assist social workers in meeting the needs of individuals and families who could benefit from genetic services.

- Garrison, W.T., & McQuiston, S. (1989). *Chronic illness during childhood and adolescence: Psychological aspects.* Newbury Park, CA: Sage Publications.

   This compact book integrates research and theory from several areas to address the scope of the problem of chronic illness and its impact on children and families. The authors describe how chronic illnesses affect child development, as well as children's concepts of health and illnesses and children's health behavior. A discussion of psychosocial functioning highlights cognitive functioning and academic performance, socioemotional functioning, and family coping. Approaches to psychosocial assessment and intervention are described. Frequent case examples enliven the text. This book provides an excellent overview of chronic illness during childhood and adolescence and is recommended for the reader interested in obtaining conceptual frameworks for understanding and intervention.

- Rolland, J.S. (1994). *Families, illness, & disability: An integrative treatment approach.* New York: Basic Books.

This book presents an influential psychosocial topology of illness that identifies four dimensions that shape the impact of serious conditions on families: onset (acute or gradual), course (progressive, constant, or relapsing), outcome (nonfatal, shortened life span, or sudden death/fatal), and degree of incapacitation (none, mild, moderate, or severe). The time phases of illnesses (crisis, chronic, and terminal) also shape the impact of serious conditions on families. Using a family systems perspective, the author provides an overview of family dynamics with chronic disorders; multigenerational experiences with illness, loss, and crisis; chronic disorders and the life cycle; family health and illness belief systems; and anticipatory loss. The book concludes with a discussion of treatment issues and interventions. The framework for identifying the demands associated with specific conditions provides a useful assessment tool. Although the book does not discuss low-income families and the vulnerability of children with chronic conditions to neglect and abuse, it is a must for readers who are familiar with family therapy and want to use a family therapy approach with families of children with chronic health conditions.

- Schild, S., & Black, R.B. (1984). *Social work and genetics: a guide for practice.* New York: The Haworth Press.

This 142-page book (plus glossary, selected review of genetic disorders, and references) clearly presents essential genetic information, including the knowledge base for social work in genetics, social and psychological issues, perspectives on social work practice with people with genetic concerns, the history and policy issues of genetic screening, and ethical and legal issues. Because it was published in 1984, some of the technical genetics information is outdated. Nonetheless, this is a handy, one-volume overview of biopsychosocial issues and genetic social work practice.

- Seligman, M., & Darling, R.B. (1997). *Ordinary families, special children: A systems approach to childhood disability* (2nd ed.). New York: Guilford Press.

Written from a systems perspective, this book is intended to assist professionals who wish to take a family-centered approach to working with families of children with disabilities. Chapters present a conceptual framework: the diagnostic crisis; adaptation during childhood and adolescence; effects on the family system, on siblings and on fathers and grandparents; cultural reactions to childhood disability and subcultural variations; professional-family interactions; and therapeutic approaches. The final chapter discusses a systems approach to planning and implementing an individualized family service plan. This highly acclaimed book is a comprehensive resource that shows professionals how to apply a social and family systems-based approach to assessment and intervention with diverse families. Although the authors do not specifically address the plight of low-income families who have children with disabilities, the principles of family-centered and comprehensive care apply.

- Weiss, J.O. (1981). Psychosocial stress in genetic disorders: A guide for social workers. *Social Work in Healthcare, 6,* 17–31.

This classic article written by a pioneer in genetic social works provides a concise overview of psychosocial issues associated with genetic disorders.

References

Amadio, C. (1989). Wrongful adoption—A new basis for litigation, another challenge for child welfare. *Journal of Law and Social Work, 1* (1), 23–30.

Andersen, P. (1997). Cues of culture: The basis of intercultural differences in nonverbal communication. In L.A. Samovar & R.E. Porter (Eds.), *Intercultural communication: A reader* (8th ed.) (pp. 244–255). Belmont, CA: Wadsworth Publishing Company.

Andrews, L.B. (1987). *Medical genetics: A legal frontier.* Chicago: American Bar Association.

Barna, L.M. (1997). Stumbling blocks in intercultural communication. In L.A. Samovar & R.E. Porter (Eds.), *Intercultural Communication: A reader* (pp. 370–378). Belmont, CA: Wadsworth Publishing Company.

Bennett, J. (1993). Definitions: Culture, ethnicity, & race. In *Readings for the Summer Institute for Intercultural Communication* (p. 2). Unpublished anthology from the Summer Institute for Intercultural Communication, Portland, Oregon, July 16–18, 1997.

Bernhardt, B., & Rauch, J.B. (1993). Genetic family histories: An aid to social work assessment. *Families in Society, 74* (4), 195–205.

Billings, P.R. (1992). Discrimination as a consequence of genetic testing. *American Journal of Human Genetics, 50,* 476–482.

Bishop, K.K. (1993). Psychosocial aspects of genetic disorders: Implications for practice. *Families in Society, 74* (4), 207–212.

Black, R.B., & Furlong, R.M. (1984). Impact of prenatal diagnosis in families. *Social Work in Health Care, 9,* 37–50.

Blair, M.B. (1996). The Uniform Adoption Act's health disclosure provisions: A model that should not be overlooked. *Family Law Quarterly, 30* (2), 427–482.

Blumberg, B.D., Golbus, M.S., & Hanson, K.H. (1974). The psychological sequelae of abortion performed for a genetic indication. *American Journal of Obstetrics and Gynecology, 122,* 799–808.

Boyle, J.S., & Andrews, M.M. (1989). *Transcultural concepts in nursing care.* Glenview, IL: Scott, Foresman/Little, Brown College Division.

Brislin, R. (1993). Understanding *culture's influence on behavior.* Orlando, FL: Holt, Rinehart and Winston, Inc.

Carrasco, M. (1999). Health care issues of children in placement: The example of foster care. In H.M. Wallace, G. Green, K.J. Jaros, L.L. Paine, & M. Story (Eds.), *Health and welfare for families in the 21st century* (pp. 197–204). Sudbury, MA: Jones and Bartlett Publishers.

Chadwick, D.L. (1992). The health and care of foster children. *APSAC Advisor, 5* (2), 3–4.

Chernoff, R.; Combs-Orme, T.; Risley-Curtiss, C.; & Heisler, A. (1994). *Assessing the health status of children entering foster care. Pediatrics, 93* (4), 594–600.

Child Welfare League of America. (1988). *Standards for adoption service* (Rev. ed.). Washington, DC: Author.

Collins, F.C. (21 May 1996). *The human genome project.* Presented at a conference, The Genetic Self, National Center for Human Genome Research, Warrenton, VA.

DeVita, P.R., & Armstrong, J.D. (1993). *Distant mirrors: America as a foreign culture.* Belmont, CA: Wadsworth Publishing Company.

DeWoody, M. (1993a). Adoption and disclosure of medical and social history. *Child Welfare, 72* (3), 195–218.

DeWoody, M. (1993b). *Adoption and disclosure: A review of the law.* Washington, DC: Child Welfare League of America.

DK illustrated Oxford dictionary. (1998). New York: Oxford University Press and DK Publishing Company.

Engel, L.W. (1993). The human genome project: History, goals and progress to date. *Archives of Pathology & Laboratory Medicine, 117* (5), 459–65.

Erikson, E.H. (1963). *Identity, youth, and crisis* (2nd ed.). New York: W.W. Norton and Company, Inc.

Ewalt, P.L.; Freeman, E.M.; Kirk, S.A.; & Poole, D.L. (Eds.). (1996). *Multicultural issues in social work.* Washington, DC: National Association of Social Workers.

Ewalt, P.L.; Freeman, E.M.; Fortune, A.E.; Poole, D.L.; & Witkins, S.L. (Eds.). (1999). *Multicultural issues in social work: Practice and research.* Washington DC: National Association of Social Workers.

Faden, R., & Kass, N.E. (1993). Genetic screening technology: Ethical issues in access to tests by employers and health insurance companies. *Journal of Social Issues, 49* (2), 75–88.

Freundlich, M., & Peterson, L. (1998). *Wrongful adoption: Law, policy, & practice.* Washington, DC: Child Welfare League of America.

Furlong, R.M., & Black, R.B. (1984). Pregnancy termination for genetic indications. *Social Work in Health Care, 10,* 17–34.

Garbarino, J.; Bookhouse, P.E.; & Authier, K.J. (1986). *Special children, special risks: The maltreatment of children with disabilities.* New York: Aldine de Gruyter.

Garver, K.L., & Garver, B. (1994). The human genome project and eugenic concerns. *American Journal of Human Genetics, 54,* 148–158.

Gary, L.C. (1974). The sickle cell controversy. *Social Work, 19,* 263–272.

Green, J.W. (1999). *Cultural awareness in the human services: A multi-ethnic approach* (3rd ed.). Boston: Allyn and Bacon.

Gudykunst, W.B. (1994). *Bridging differences: Effective intergroup communication* (2nd ed.). Thousand Oaks: CA: SAGE Publications.

Gudykunst, W.B., & Kim, Y.Y. (1997). *Communicating with strangers: An approach to intercultural communication* (3rd ed.). Boston: McGraw-Hill.

Guyer, M.F., & Collins, F.C. (1993). The human genome project and the future of medicine. *American Journal of Diseases of Children, 147* (11), 1145–1152.

Hochman, G., & Huston, A. (1994). *Providing background information to adoptive parents.* Rockville, MD: National Adoption Clearinghouse.

Hoopes, D.S., & Pusch, M.D. (1997). Definition of terms. In *Foundations of intercultural communications* (p. 53). Unpublished anthology from the Summer Institute for Intercultural Communication, Portland, Oregon, July 16–18, 1997.

Kadushin, A., & Martin, J.A. (1988). *Child welfare services* (4th ed.). New York: McMillan Publishing Company.

Kevles, D.J. (1985). *In the name of eugenics: Genetics and the uses of human heredity.* New York: Alfred A. Knopf.

Kim, Y.Y. (1997). Adapting to a new culture. In L.A. Samovar & R.E. Porter (Eds.), *Intercultural communication* (8th ed.) (pp. 404–416). Belmont, CA: Wadsworth Publishing Company.

Kluckhohn, F., & Strodtbeck, F. (1961). *Variations in value orientations.* Westport, CN: Greenwood Press.

Kohls, L.R. (1988). The values Americans live by. In P.L. Thompson & J.M. Bennett (Eds.), *Concepts of intercultural communication.* Unpublished anthology. Portland, OR: The Intercultural Communication Institute.

Kopels, S. (1995). Wrongful adoptions: Litigation and liability. *Families in Society, 76* (1), 20–29.

Lamport, A.T. (1988). The genetics of secrecy in adoption, artificial insemination and in vitro fertilization. *American Journal of Law and Medicine, 14* (1), 109–124.

Lecca, P.J.; Quervalú, I.; Nunes, J.V.; & Gonzales, H.F. (1998). *Cultural competency in health, social, and human services: Directions for the twenty-first century.* New York & London: Garland Publishing, Inc.

Lustig, M.W., & Koester, J. (1996). *Intercultural competence: Interpersonal communication across cultures* (2nd ed.). New York: HarperCollins College Publishers.

McGuffin, P., & Murray, R. (1991). The new genetics of mental illness. *Butterworth-Heinemann Medical Journal, 38,* 949–952.

McGuffin, P.; Owens, M.J.; O'Donovan, M.C.; Thapar, A.; & Gottesman, I.L. (1994). *Seminars in psychiatric genetics.* Washington, DC: American Psychiatric Press.

McKusick, V. (1999). *Online mendalian inheritance in man.* Available online at www.ncbi.nlm.nih.gov.omim. Bethesda, MD: National Center for Biotechnology Information.

A National Adoption Strategic Plan. (1996). Roundtable. *Journal of the National Resource Center for Special Needs Adoption, 10* (2), 1–5.

Natowicz, M.R.; Alper, J.K.; & Alper, J.S. (1992). Genetic discrimination and the law. *American Journal of Human Genetics, 50,* 465–475.

Omenn, G.S.; Hall, J.G.; & Hansen, K.D. (1980). Genetic counseling for adoptees at risk for specific inherited disorders. *American Journal of Medical Genetics, 5,* 157–164.

Paige, M. (July 18, 1997). *Foundations of intercultural communication.* Lecture delivered at Summer Institute for Intercultural Communication, Portland, Oregon.

Pinkney, D.S. (1994). American's sickest children. *Youth Law News, 15* (6), 15–18.

Pyeritz, R.E. (1989). Assessing the role of genes in diseases of adulthood. *Maryland Medical Journal, 38,* 949–952.

Rauch, J.B.; Sarno, C.; & Simpson, S. (1991). Screening for affective disorders. *Families in Society, 72* (10), 602–609.

Rauch, J.B.; North, C.; Rowe, C.L.; & Risley-Curtiss, C. (1993). *Diversity competence: A learning guide.* Baltimore: University of Maryland at Baltimore, School of Social Work.

Reilly, P. (1977). *Genetics, law, and social policy.* Cambridge, MA: Harvard University Press.

Rimoin, D.L.; Connor, J.M.; & Pyeritz, R.E. (1996). *Emery & Rimoin's principles and practices of medical genetics* (3rd ed.). New York: Churchill-Livingstone.

Robinson, A. (1988). Genetics and the health professional. In J. Scott (Ed.), *Genetic applications: A health perspective* (pp. 1–3). Lawrence, KS: Learner Managed Designs.

Roland, A. (1994). Identity, self, and individualism in multicultural perspective. In E.P. Salett & D.R. Koslow (Eds.), *Race, ethnicity, and self: Identity in multicultural perspective* (pp. 11–23). Washington, DC: National Multicultural Institute.

Rolland, J.S. (1994). *Families, illness, and disability: An integrative treatment model.* New York: Basic Books.

Samovar, L.A.; Porter, R.E.; & Stefani, L.A. (1998). *Communication between cultures* (3rd ed.). Belmont, CA: Wadsworth Publishing Company.

Schild, S. (1973). Social work with genetic problems. *Health and Social Work, 2,* 58–77.

Schild, S., & Black, R.B. (1984). *Social work and genetics: A guide for practice.* New York: Haworth Press.

Scott, R.B. (1970). Health care priority and sickle cell anemia. *Journal of the American Medical Association, 214,* 731–734.

Stewart, E.C., & Bennett, M.J. (1991). *American cultural patterns: A cross-cultural perspective* (Rev. ed.). Yarmouth, MD: Intercultural Press.

Turnball, A.P., & Turnball, H.R., III (1985). Developing independence in adolescents with disabilities. *Journal of Adolescent Health Care, 6* (2), 108–124.

Turnball, A.P., & Turnball, H.R., III, with J.A. Summers, M.J. Brotherson, & H.A. Benson. (1997). *Families, professionals and exceptionality: A special partnership* (3rd ed.). Upper Saddle River, NJ: Merrill Publishing Company.

Uniform Adoption Act. (1994). *Uniform Laws, Annotated. Vol. 9, Part I. 1998 Supplementary Pamphlet.* St. Paul, MN: West Group Publishers.

U.S. Department of Education. (1992). *Summary of existing legislation affecting people with disabilities.* (Publication No. ED/OSERS 92-8). Washington, DC: U.S. Government Printing Office.

U.S. General Accounting Office. (1995). *Foster care: Health needs of many young children are unknown and unmet.* Technical Report. Gaithersburg, MD: Author.

White, J.C. (1974). Screening programs for sickle cell disease. *Social Work, 19* (3), 273–278.

Yum, J.O. (1997). The impact of Confucianism on interpersonal relationships and communication patterns in East Asia. In L.A. Samovar & R.E. Porter (Eds.), *Intercultural communication: A reader* (8th ed.) (pp. 78–88). Belmont, CA: Wadsworth Publishing Company.

About the Authors

Karen Eanet, M.S., is a genetic counselor at the Harvey Institute for Genetics at Greater Baltimore Medical Center, Baltimore, Maryland. An adult adoptee, she has extensive experience in providing genetics training to child welfare workers and to adoptive parents.

Julia B. Rauch, M.S.W., Ph.D., LCSW-C, is professor and director of the Center for Maternal and Child Health Social Work Education at the School of Social Work, University of Maryland-Baltimore. She has a long-standing interest in genetics and in genetics training for social workers.

Notes

Notes

Notes

Notes

Notes

Notes

Notes